Cambridge Elements ≡

Elements in Criminology
edited by
David Weisburd
George Mason University, Virginia
Hebrew University of Jerusalem

TESTING CRIMINAL CAREER THEORIES IN BRITISH AND AMERICAN LONGITUDINAL STUDIES

John F. MacLeod
Cambridge University Institute of Criminology

David P. Farrington
Cambridge University Institute of Criminology

CAMBRIDGE
UNIVERSITY PRESS

CAMBRIDGE
UNIVERSITY PRESS

University Printing House, Cambridge CB2 8BS, United Kingdom

One Liberty Plaza, 20th Floor, New York, NY 10006, USA

477 Williamstown Road, Port Melbourne, VIC 3207, Australia

314–321, 3rd Floor, Plot 3, Splendor Forum, Jasola District Centre,
New Delhi – 110025, India

103 Penang Road, #05–06/07, Visioncrest Commercial, Singapore 238467

Cambridge University Press is part of the University of Cambridge.

It furthers the University's mission by disseminating knowledge in the pursuit of
education, learning, and research at the highest international levels of excellence.

www.cambridge.org
Information on this title: www.cambridge.org/9781009018067
DOI: 10.1017/9781009039628

First published 2022

A catalogue record for this publication is available from the British Library.

ISBN 978-1-009-01806-7 Paperback
ISSN 2633-3341 (online)
ISSN 2633-3333 (print)

Testing Criminal Career Theories in British and American Longitudinal Studies

Elements in Criminology

DOI: 10.1017/9781009039628
First published online: May 2022

John F. MacLeod
Cambridge University Institute of Criminology

David P. Farrington
Cambridge University Institute of Criminology

Author for correspondence: John F. MacLeod, jfmacl83@gmail.com

Abstract: Most criminological theories aim to explain and predict only the total prevalence of offending. They are not truly scientific since they do not yield exact quantitative predictions of key criminal career features such as the prevalence and frequency of offending of a cohort at different ages (the age–crime curve). The main aim of this Element is to make progress towards more scientific criminal career theories. A simple theory is described based on measures of *risk* (the probability of reoffending after each crime) and *rate* (the frequency of offending by offenders). Three categories of offenders are identified: *high-risk/high-rate (HH)*, *high-risk/low-rate (HL)*, and *low-risk/low-rate (LL)*. It is demonstrated that this theory accurately predicts key criminal career features – the age–crime curve, the probability of recidivism, and time intervals between offences – in three data sets: the Offenders Index (OI) (national English cohort data), the British Cambridge Study in Delinquent Development (CSDD), and the American Pittsburgh Youth Study (PYS). The theory is then extended in the CSDD and PYS by identifying early risk factors that predict the three categories of offenders. Criminological theorists are encouraged to try to replicate and build on our research in order to develop scientific theories that yield quantitative predictions of key criminal career features.

Keywords: criminological theories, criminal careers, types of offenders, risk factors, mathematical models

ISBNs: 9781009018067 (PB), 9781009039628 (OC)
ISSNs: 2633-3341 (online), 2633-3333 (print)

Contents

1 Introduction

Unlike in the physical sciences, theories in criminology (as in the other social and behavioural sciences) rarely derive or test exact quantitative predictions. In a true science, exact quantitative predictions are derived and tested empirically. Most criminological theories aim to explain and predict (qualitatively rather than quantitatively) only the total prevalence of offending. In developmental and life-course criminology (see e.g. Farrington, 2005), theories also aim to specify the extent to which total prevalence is influenced by classic individual, family, and socio-economic risk factors. However, it is highly desirable to propose theories that also explain and predict important criminal career features such as the age–crime curve, the probability of recidivism after each offence, and time intervals between offences. The main aim of this Element is to make progress towards truly scientific criminology by deriving and testing exact quantitative predictions about key criminal career features from simple theories. We hope that criminologists will build on our simple theories to develop and test more complex theories (e.g. incorporating risk and protective factors) that make exact quantitative predictions.

1.1 The Moffitt Theory

As an example of a criminological theory that does not yield quantitative predictions but does attempt to explain the age–crime curve, consider the, very influential, developmental taxonomy theory of Moffitt (1993). She aimed to reconcile two apparently incongruous facts about offending, namely that it shows impressive continuity over time but that its prevalence changes dramatically at different ages, peaking in the teenage years. She proposed that there were two distinct categories of individuals, namely life-course-persistent (LCP) and adolescence-limited (AL) offenders, who differed in kind rather than in degree.

Moffitt stated that LCP offenders were influenced by many classic risk factors, including pregnancy problems of their mothers, neuropsychological deficits including impulsivity and inattention, cognitive deficits including low intelligence and attainment, poor child-rearing including low parental warmth and inconsistent discipline, disrupted families, and socio-economic deprivation. In contrast, AL offenders were motivated by the gap between their biological and social maturity (e.g. they wanted material goods and status but could not achieve them legitimately during adolescence), and they were influenced by their LCP peers ('social mimicry'). They ceased offending in young adulthood because they could then achieve their aims legitimately when they had social skills and no cognitive deficits (e.g. they did not have low intelligence or low academic attainment).

This theory is undoubtedly one of the most important and most researched criminological theories. Moffitt (2018) and McGee and Moffitt (2019) have summarized developments in the quarter-century since the theory was propounded. Generally, the theory has held up well, but there have been concerns with new categories of offenders such as low-level chronics and adult-onset offenders and also with abstainers who refrain from offending entirely.

While this theory is excellent in many ways, it does not make or test exact quantitative predictions about such basic parameters as the prevalence of LCP and AL offenders and their frequency of offending at different ages. Also, the theory does not specify the exact quantitative impact of risk factors on types of offenders. Moffitt (1993) says that about 5 per cent, or at least less than 10 per cent, of males would be LCP offenders (at all ages combined), while a much higher fraction (peaking at over 60 per cent in her figure 3) would be AL offenders. However, she has not yet attempted to quantify her theory and show to what extent it can predict actual criminal career data (e.g. the number of crimes committed at different ages by a birth cohort).

1.2 Group-Based Trajectory Modelling

Moffitt's theory has been tested empirically using group-based trajectory modelling (GBTM). This was first used by Nagin and Land (1993), who stated explicitly that 'Analyses reported herein are also designed to test for the existence of the sorts of distinctive offending trajectories predicted by Moffitt's theory' (pp. 328–329). GBTM fits criminal career data by assuming that individuals commit crimes according to a Poisson process (i.e. randomly over time). They assume that Ln(lambda), where lambda is the individual's underlying frequency of offending, depends on time-stable characteristics of the individual as well as age and (age-squared). It was important to control for these time-stable characteristics because Nagin and Farrington (1992) previously concluded that the link between past and future offending was largely driven by persistent heterogeneity (the persistence over time of individual differences in underlying criminal potential) rather than by state dependence (the effect of past offending on future offending). Nagin and Land (1993) analysed Cambridge Study in Delinquent Development (CSDD, discussed later) data up to age thirty-two and found three categories of offenders (high-rate chronics, low-rate chronics, and AL) plus non-offenders, in fitting criminal career data. These analyses were later extended by Nagin et al. (1995).

While GBTM is a very important method, it is important to point out that it is a method of fitting criminal career data rather than a criminological theory. For example, there is no theoretical reason advanced to explain why the frequency of offending should depend on (age-squared). Skardhamar (2010, p. 299), in a critique of GBTM, stated that it is 'a "theory-free method" (Moffitt, 2006, p. 581), one that allows us to identify unobservable groups that "emerge from data itself" (Nagin, 2005, p. 2) rather than being assumed *a priori*'. Skardhamar (2010) further argued that, even when no groups exist in reality and the data are truly continuous, GBTM will reveal several categories of offenders.

Nagin and Tremblay (2005) were careful to point out that 'trajectory groups, like all statistical models, are not literal depictions of reality. They are meant only as a convenient statistical approximation' (p. 882). They further stated (p. 887) that the idea that individuals actually belong to a trajectory group is a 'misconception' and that 'the number of groups and the shape of each group's trajectory are not fixed realities' (p. 888). Indeed, Farrington et al. (2013) documented how membership of the trajectories changed in the CSDD as the follow-up age was extended from 24 to 32 to 40 to 48 and finally to 56. Nagin and Tremblay (2005, p. 898) summarized that 'it is important for users and consumers of the analyses [to] remember that individuals do not actually belong to a trajectory group, that the number of trajectory groups in a sample is not immutable, and that individuals do not follow the group-level trajectory in lockstep'.

GBTM has advanced knowledge greatly, but it is not a criminological theory. We now turn to very simple criminological theories (criminal career models) that yield quantitative predictions that can be tested in criminal career data.

1.3 Criminal Career Models

Blumstein et al. (1985) attempted to predict observed recidivism probabilities in four cohort studies. Their key assumption was that each offender had a constant probability of persisting after each offence. They found that observed recidivism probabilities and, more generally, the distribution of offences over offenders could be predicted by a model that partitioned each sample into three subgroups: *innocents*, who had no offending record; *desisters*, who had a low recidivism probability; and *persisters*, who had a high recidivism probability. The observed aggregate recidivism probability increased after each arrest because the desisters tended to drop out and leave behind a sample composed increasingly of the persisters.

Blumstein et al. (1985) then applied their mathematical model (of innocents, desisters, and persisters) to the CSDD data. The best fit to the recidivism probabilities in the CSDD was obtained by assuming that the probability of persisting after each conviction was 0.87 for persisters and 0.57 for desisters.

The proportion of first offenders who were persisters was 0.28, while the fraction of the sample who were innocents was 0.67. Persisters and desisters differed in their a priori probabilities of persisting, not in their a posteriori number of convictions (as chronics did). This model fitted the data very accurately.

Interestingly, the number of empirically predicted chronics among the offenders (37 'high-risk' offenders with four or more out of seven childhood risk factors) was similar to the predicted number of persisters (36.7) according to the model. Remarkably, the individual process of dropping out of crime by the predicted chronics in the empirical data closely matched the aggregate dropout process for persisters predicted by the model with parameters estimated from aggregate recidivism data. Therefore, the high-risk offenders might be viewed as the identified persisters. This analysis shows the important distinction between prospective empirical predictions (e.g. high-risk offenders), underlying theoretical categories (e.g. persisters), and retrospectively measured outcomes (e.g. chronics).

Barnett and Lofaso (1985) analysed the Philadelphia cohort data of Wolfgang et al. (1972). In contrast to Blumstein et al. (1985), they did not focus on the probability of persistence, but rather on the frequency of offending. They aimed to predict the individual offending frequency (the average number of offences per offender per year) rather than the number of offences committed. They assumed that offences were committed probabilistically (at random) over time, which meant that offenders committed crimes according to a stationary Poisson process (with a constant mean rate). They found that the best predictor of the future individual offending frequency (crimes per year) was the past individual offending frequency.

Barnett et al. (1987) then combined the approaches of Blumstein et al. (1985) and Barnett and Lofaso (1985). They analysed conviction data from the CSDD and aimed to predict the number of offences of each person at each age as well as time intervals between crimes. They tested several models of criminal careers containing two key parameters: (1) p = the probability that an offender terminates the criminal career after the kth conviction; for any given offender, p is assumed to be constant for all values of k, and (2) μ = the individual offending frequency per year, or the annual rate at which the offender sustains convictions while free during the active career. The individual offending frequency cannot be estimated from aggregate data simply by dividing the number of convictions at each age by the number of offenders at each age because some active offenders who have embarked on a criminal career may not be convicted at a particular age.

Barnett et al. (1987) found that models assuming that all offenders had the same p and μ did not fit the data and therefore assumed that there were two categories of offenders: 'frequents' and 'occasionals'. Each category had its own value of p and μ, which were assumed to be constant over time. They found that the model that best fitted the data had the following parameters: μ_F (conviction rate of frequents per year) = 1.14, μ_o (conviction rate of occasionals per year) = 0.41, p_F (termination probability of frequents after each conviction) = 0.10, p_o (termination probability of occasionals after each conviction) = 0.33, and α (fraction of frequents compared to occasionals) = 0.43. Thus, 43 per cent of the offenders were frequents, and this group had a higher individual offending frequency and a lower probability of terminating their criminal careers after each conviction. Barnett et al. (1987) did not suggest that there were in reality only two categories of offenders, but rather that it was possible to fit the conviction data (the number of convictions of each offender at each age) accurately using a simple model that assumed only two categories.

Barnett et al. (1987) basically showed that a very simple criminological theory, focussing only on the frequency of offending and the probability of termination after each conviction, could produce accurate quantitative predictions of the number of offences of each person at each age and of time intervals between crimes. Furthermore, Barnett et al. (1989) carried out a test of the predictive validity of this model using the CSDD data. The model was developed on conviction data between the tenth and twenty-fifth birthdays and tested on conviction data between the twenty-fifth and thirtieth birthdays. The aim was to predict the number of reoffenders, the identities of reoffenders, the number of reconvictions, the age at the first reconviction, and the time intervals between reconvictions in this follow-up period. Generally, the model performed well.

These very simple quantitative theories are the starting point for our Element. Surprisingly, since the 1980s, there have been very few attempts to develop and test simple theories of the type developed by Blumstein and his colleagues (see Farrington et al., 2016). An exception is the book, *Explaining Criminal Careers*, by MacLeod et al. (2012). Some key features of this book are described in Section 2.

1.4 The 'Great Debate' in Criminology

Rocque et al. (2016) pointed out that the 'great debate' in criminology focussed on the explanation of the age–crime curve, which is clearly a crucial criminological phenomenon. This debate was between Gottfredson and Hirschi on one side and Blumstein and his collaborators on the other side.

In the landmark report of the US National Academy of Sciences Panel on Criminal Career research, Blumstein et al. (1986) emphasized the need to distinguish different features of criminal careers. Farrington (1992, p. 521) summarized these key features: 'A criminal career has a beginning (onset), an end (desistance), and a career length in between (duration). Only a certain proportion of the population (prevalence) has a criminal career and commits offences. During their careers, offenders commit offences at a certain rate (frequency) while they are at risk of offending in the community (i.e. not incarcerated or hospitalized)'.

Hirschi and Gottfredson (1983) argued that the age–crime curve was 'invariant' regardless of sex, race, country, time period, or crime type. They stated that crime rates decreased with age (after the peak) because of 'inexorable ageing' and decreases in biological factors such as energy, physical strength, and testosterone (in males). They further argued that criminal career research and longitudinal studies were not needed because the correlates of offending were the same at all ages. Gottfredson and Hirschi (1986) contended that all criminal career features reflected the single underlying construct of 'criminal propensity'; when this was high, the onset of offending was early, the desistance of offending was late, the duration of offending was high, and the frequency of offending was high. Therefore, prevalence and frequency both reflected criminal propensity; the causes of offending were the same at all ages; and the causes of onset and desistance were the same.

Blumstein et al. (1988a, 1988b) contended that these arguments were incorrect. For example, in the CSDD, they reported that the predictors of conviction (onset) were generally different from the predictors of reconviction (persistence). Earlier, Farrington (1986) showed that the age–crime curve was not invariant but varied over time, place, sex, and crime type and that it reflected prevalence rather than frequency. Later, Farrington and Hawkins (1991) in the CSDD and Loeber et al. (1991) in the Pittsburgh Youth Study (PYS, discussed later) showed in more detail that different criminal career features had different predictors.

Rocque et al. (2016, p. 4) concluded that:

> More recent research on age and crime has failed to unequivocally adjudicate these two positions, but it seems as if the 'criminal career' camp has garnered more support. In other words, more recent research on age and crime has shown that there is a benefit to longitudinal methodologies, that something is to be gained by examining different parts of the criminal career, and that the relationship between age and crime is not entirely invariant.

We believe that Blumstein and his collaborators are correct. Nevertheless, most criminological theories are still concordant with the Gottfredson–Hirschi approach in only trying to explain influences on the prevalence of offending, not influences on the onset, persistence, frequency, desistance, or duration.

Furthermore, most criminological theories are very complex. We believe that a simple theory that explains and predicts a wide range of results is preferable. This point is also made in Agent-Based Modelling, which aims to develop the simplest possible theory and model for a simulation that will provide a realistic set of outcomes (see Weisburd et al., 2017). We hope that our Element will stimulate more adequate, more scientific, and more quantitative theories that aim to explain criminal career features.

In this Element, we use two key parameters – the frequency of offending and the probability of reoffending – to define categories of offenders and investigate the extent to which this simple theory fits criminal career data in two longitudinal studies: the British CSDD (Section 3) and the American PYS (Section 5). The accuracy of predictions is quite remarkable. We then go beyond these simple theories to investigate which childhood risk factors predict categories of offenders in the CSDD (Section 4) and the PYS (Section 6). These analyses suggest how the simple theories might be extended to explain and predict a wide variety of criminal career data. We hope that our analyses will encourage criminologists to formulate and test truly scientific theories that lead to quantitative predictions about how key risk factors influence key criminal career features such as the number of offenders and offences in a cohort at each age. In turn, we hope that more accurate quantitative scientific theories of criminal behaviour will lead to more effective prevention and intervention strategies.

2 The Offenders Index (OI) and the *Risk/Rate* Model

2.1 The MacLeod et al. Analyses

MacLeod et al. (2012) proposed a quantitative theory of criminal careers based on a detailed analysis of official conviction data extracted from the UK Home Office Offenders Index (OI). The mathematical models derived from this theory were shown to fit both longitudinal and cross-sectional conviction data very well. MacLeod et al. also identified the theoretical offender categories from psychological and behavioural data from the Offender Assessment System (OASys) developed and used by the prison and probation services of England and Wales. In this Element, we test this theory using independently collected conviction and assessment data from the CSDD and the PYS. 'Offences' always refer to offences leading to convictions.

The OI was created in 1963 and contains records obtained from courts in England and Wales for each court appearance resulting in a conviction for one or more 'standard list' offences. The 'standard list' includes all offences that may be tried in the Crown Court (more serious indictable and 'either-way' offences), as well as the more serious of the offences that can only be tried in the

Magistrates' Courts. The most common types of offence are theft, violence, vandalism, fraud, and drug use. The definition of 'standard list' has changed during the period covered by the OI, with offences being added to or removed from the list, but the MacLeod et al. analyses were based on the definition used in the early 1990s. Cohort samples, comprising all court appearance records for individuals born in one of four weeks during the cohort years of 1953, 1958, 1963, 1968, and 1973, were extracted in 1992/1993, 1999/2000, and 2006 (see Ministry of Justice Statistics Bulletin, 2010). The records of the different convictions for each individual were linked together to form individual OI criminal career histories. The 1992/1993 extracts were used as the basis for the MacLeod et al. analyses, with the 1953 cohort updated to 1999 at age 46. The 1953 cohort is directly comparable to the CSDD cohort, as most of the latter's males were born in 1953.

In the MacLeod et al. analysis, for each individual in the OI cohort, court appearances were labelled with a sequence number, 1 for the first court appearance, 2 for the second, and so on. Conviction records were restricted to principal convictions, coding only the most serious offence dealt with in the court appearance, and a histogram of the count of individuals with n or more principal convictions was constructed. Plotting this histogram, with a linear x-axis (conviction number n) and a logarithmic y-axis (number of court appearances), it is clear, from Figure 1 (MacLeod et al. 2012, figure 2.3, p. 29), that the data points for $n > 6$ lie on a straight line with slope Log (p_1).

It is also clear that the residuals from that line for $n < 6$ also fall on a straight line with a much steeper slope Log (p_2). From this graphical analysis, the 'dual *risk* recidivism model' was derived Eq. (1) (MacLeod et al. 2012, Equation 2.4, p. 30)

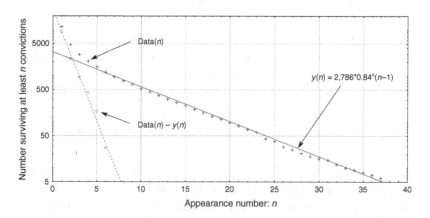

Figure 1 Number of individuals with n or more convictions in the OI 1953 cohort

$$\mathbf{Y}(n) = \mathrm{A} * \left(\mathrm{a} * \mathrm{p}_1^{(n-1)} + (1 - \mathrm{a}) * \mathrm{p}_2^{(n-1)} \right), \tag{1}$$

where:

$\mathbf{Y}(n)$ is the number of individuals with at least n convictions,

$\mathbf{A}$ is the total number of individuals in the cohort with at least one conviction,

$\mathbf{a}$ is the proportion of individuals in the *high-risk* (of reconviction) category,

$\mathbf{p_1}$ Is the *high-risk* probability of reconviction, and

$\mathbf{p_2}$ is the *low-risk* probability of reconviction.

The model parameters were estimated for the five longitudinal OI cohort samples and for a 1997 OI cross-sectional sentencing sample. All samples had the same dual *risk* structure, and parameter values were found to be consistent, allowing for the reducing follow-up periods. This model also provided a convincing explanation for the increasing probability of reconviction with conviction number in the early stages of criminal careers. This increasing probability was due to the more rapidly reducing number of *low-risk* individuals as conviction number increased.

A similar analysis of inter-conviction times, using the numbers of offenders surviving conviction-free up to time t from the previous conviction, was used to identify the 'dual-*rate* survival time model', Eq. (2) (MGF, 2012, Equation 2.8, p. 35). Survival times were used to smooth out random variations in the inter-conviction time data.

$$S(t) = S_0 * \left(b^* e^{-\lambda_1 * t} + (1 - b) * e^{-\lambda_2 * t} \right), \tag{2}$$

where:

$S(t)$ is the number of offenders surviving conviction-free, up to time t from the previous conviction,

S_0 is the total number of inter-conviction times in the data,

λ_1, λ_2 are the mean numbers of convictions per year for the *high-rate* and *low-rate* categories of offenders, respectively, and

b is the proportion of inter-conviction times attributed to the *high-rate* category of offenders.

The parameter values were estimated for the above-mentioned OI cohort samples. The same dual-rate structure was found, and the parameter estimates were again consistent across cohorts allowing for the length of respective follow-up periods. For the 1953 birth cohort, with the longest follow-up period, the parameters were: $a = 0.237$, $p_1 = 0.840$, $p_2 = 0.313$, $b = 0.565$,

$\lambda_1 = 0.859$, and $\lambda_2 = 0.212$. All the OI cohorts included both male and female offenders.

In the MacLeod et al. analyses, due to the lack of detailed information, immigration and emigration were assumed to balance out or at least, along with death, were assumed to have limited impact on the underlying processes. Also, the time offenders spent in prison, although clearly important at the individual level, was not taken into account in the analysis for several reasons. First, only sentence length had been recorded on the OI, so there was no allowance for remission, parole, partial suspension of sentence, or time spent on remand. Second, inter-conviction time distributions for individuals with custodial sentences were not significantly different from those of similar offenders with supervisory disposals. Lastly, half the total sentence length (to allow for remission) for all the cohorts represents less than 2 per cent of the sum of active career lengths. Again, it was assumed that time in custody had only a limited impact on the underlying distributions. It should be pointed out that the average time served in England and Wales is much less than in the USA. For example, the average time served for robbery in England and Wales in 1997 was 19.3 months, whereas the average time served for robbery in the USA in 1996 was 37.4 months (Farrington et al., 2004).

Because Eqs. (1) and (2) fitted the data of five independent cohort samples and one cross-sectional sample very well, this suggests that these are not only good models of the data but also a good representation of the processes generating the data. It is, however, important that the parameters of the models have real-world meaning and that the processes described are plausible in the context of the individuals and events creating the data. Arbitrary equations (e.g. quadratic, cubic, or higher-order polynomials) can fit continuously varying data as closely as we please.[1] For the equations to be theoretically useful, a plausible theory is required that generates the same equations and parameters that relate to measurable quantities.

2.2 The MacLeod et al. Theory

The underlying theory developed in MacLeod et al. (2012) is a categorized theory of criminal convictions. A basic legal premise of criminal convictions is that individuals are responsible for their actions and that they decide to commit or not to commit a criminal act. There are exceptions to criminal responsibility, principally if a person is underage or of unsound mind at the time of an offence. In this theory, it is proposed that individuals are more or less inclined to break

---

[1] Quote by physicist Dyson Freeman: 'Johnny von Neumann used to say, with four parameters I can fit an elephant, and with five I can make him wiggle his trunk'.

the law, depending in part on their moral values and in part on the perceived benefits and/or costs of the act in question. Moral values are important in some criminological theories (e.g. Wikstrom & Treiber, 2019). They may be genetically influenced but are primarily learned in childhood and modified by later-life experiences. The benefit-to-costs balance will be influenced by the circumstances at the time and place of a potential crime. For example, in their computer simulation of hot spots policing, Weisburd et al. (2017) characterize the decision to commit a robbery by a criminally motivated individual as depending on the existence of a suitable victim, the absence of deterrence by police or other citizens, and the perceived rewards and risks. A person's inclination to offend will increase as moral inhibitions decline. Where inclination is greater, more advantages will be taken of opportunities and more circumstances will be conducive to committing a crime. In other words, crime is assumed to arise from the combination of inclination and opportunity. In consequence, criminal acts may appear to be random and probabilistic.

As another theoretical example, the Integrated Cognitive Antisocial Potential (ICAP) theory distinguishes between long-term between-individual differences in antisocial potential, which develop as a result of early experiences and risk factors, and short-term within-individual variations in antisocial potential, which result from short-term energising factors (e.g. drunkenness and peer influence) and criminal opportunities (see Farrington, 2020a). Whether a person commits a crime in a criminal opportunity is assumed to depend on assessments of subjective costs, benefits, and probabilities of outcomes. Thus, this theory explains the development of long-term moral values (antisocial potential) and the short-term commission of crimes (e.g. why crimes are committed at 11 p.m. on a Friday rather than at 9 a.m. on a Monday).

The propositions of the MacLeod et al. theory were as follows:

1. Convicted persons can be divided into two *risk* categories, each with a constant but different probability of reconviction after each conviction.
2. Convicted persons can be divided into two *rate* categories, each with a constant but different probability of conviction in a given time interval. This assumption directly implies that for each *rate* category, the rate of conviction is constant, and inter-conviction times are exponentially distributed, with constant but different means.
3. These two propositions generate three[2] *risk/rate* categories: *HH, HL*, and *LL*.

---

[2] The potential fourth category, low-risk/high-rate, is not included as there is no evidence of its existence in the data.

These propositions, however, cannot account for the increase in crime during adolescence. Indeed, projecting inter-conviction times and recidivism probabilities backwards to age 10, the minimum age of criminal responsibility in England and Wales, suggested that the highest prevalence of offending would be at age 10 and that many more convictions would occur during the teenage years than are observed. Nagin and Tremblay (1999), with a sample of over 1,000 Canadian boys from age 6 to 15, conducted a trajectory analysis (fitting quadratic equations in age) of three externalising antisocial behaviours: physical aggression, oppositional behaviour, and hyperactivity. They found that for all the behaviours, each of the trajectory groups showed approximately constant or declining trajectories during early adolescence. With this in mind, the MacLeod et al. theory proposes that criminal behaviour is an extension of antisocial behaviour patterns.

In the theory, two factors are assumed to reduce officially recognized criminality during adolescence: the limited capacity of younger offenders to harm and the greater societal tolerance of antisocial acts by younger offenders. At age 10, it is unlikely that playground fights, minor vandalism, or petty theft would involve the police, let alone reach the criminal courts. As age increases, the outcomes of antisocial acts are likely to become more serious, and more formal action will be taken, leading to formal police reprimands, warnings and cautions, and eventually prosecution in the courts (as illustrated in Figures 3.5 a, b, c, and d, in MGF, 2012, pp. 57–58). During this early process, some antisocial individuals may well modify their behaviour in order to avoid criminal convictions, which means that some individuals with early indications of deviant behaviour and high criminal propensity would not face conviction in later life. These are the false positives in the prospective identification procedures described later in this Element.

To take account of these early processes, two further propositions of the MacLeod et al. theory are therefore needed to model the relationship between crime and age:

4. The rise in crime during adolescence reflects both the increasing capacity for harm and changing societal attitudes to antisocial behaviour with age.
5. The probability of capture and conviction increases once an offender is known to the police.

2.3 The Age–Crime Curve

The derivation of the survival to first conviction model is described in MacLeod et al. 2012, pp. 59–60. Eq. (3) (MacLeod et al. 2012, Equation 3.4) provides a mathematical description of the combined effect of propositions 2, 4, and 5 on a *rate* category. The theory assumes that the processes governing survival to first conviction are the same for all offenders, and thus, the survival models for *high-* and *low-rate* categories of offenders differ only in λ, the rate of conviction[3] parameter. The complete model is made up of the sum of two components, one for each of the *high-* and *low-rate* categories (i.e. $S_f(age)_{high} + S_f(age)_{low}$).

$$S_f(age) = C * (1 + e^{\alpha * (age-c)})^{-\frac{P_f * \lambda}{\alpha}}, \tag{3}$$

where:

$S_f(age)$ is the number of offenders surviving to a given age (without conviction),

α is the slope of the rise in crime transition (i.e. the rate at which the number convicted increases in the age–crime curve),[4]

c is the midpoint age of the rise in crime transition,

P_f is the relative probability of a first conviction,[5]

λ is the *rate* parameter for reconvictions, and

C is the number of offenders in the *rate* category who will be convicted in their lifetime.

Differentiating the survival model (Eq. (3)) with respect to *age* yields an expression for the annual number of first convictions at each age, $y_1(age)$, shown in Eq. (4) (MacLeod et al. 2012, equation 3.5, p. 60):[6]

$$y_1(age) = C * \left(1 + e^{\alpha*(age-c)}\right)^{-\frac{P_f*\lambda+\alpha}{\alpha}} * P_f * \lambda * e^{\alpha*(age-c)}. \tag{4}$$

Having an explicit function for the age profile at the first conviction (Eq. (4)) enables the age / conviction profile for all reconvictions to be calculated. The differential equation (Eq. (5)) uses the number of first convictions $y_1(age)$, the recidivism *risk* parameter p, and the reconviction *rate* parameter λ for each of the *risk/rate* categories to make the calculation:

$$\frac{d}{dt}y_{r>1}(age) = p * \lambda * y_1(age) - (1 - p) * \lambda * y_{r>1}(age), \tag{5}$$

where for each of the *risk/rate* categories:

---

[3] It is also assumed that the rate of conviction is directly related to the rate of offending.

[4] The slope (α) reflects the increasing capacity for harm and hardening societal attitudes to antisocial behaviour with age.

[5] The relative probability takes account of informal and official actions, not resulting in a conviction, which are often applied on a first or second offence.

[6] Please note that there is a '$+\alpha$' in the numerator of the exponent of the second term on the right-hand side of Eq. 4: this was missing in MacLeod et al. 2012, equation 3.5.

p is the reconviction probability,

$y_{r>1}$ is the annual number of offenders reconvicted, and

λ is the reconviction *rate* parameter.

Figure 2 shows the age at first conviction profile for the OI 1997 sentencing sample data with the fitted curve and the $\pm 2\sigma$ confidence bounds. The data points are at 3-month intervals in age and extend from age 10 to age 72 (MacLeod et al. 2012, Figure 3.9, p. 64).

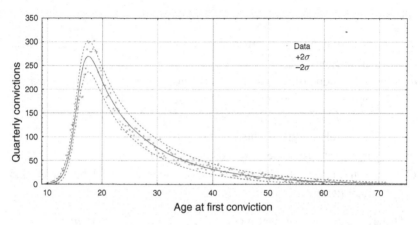

Figure 2 Age at first conviction profile for OI 1977 sentencing sample

Solving Eqs. (4) and (5) numerically, summing the results over each of the *risk/rate* categories, and substituting the result into Eq. (6) give the age–crime curve for all convictions, y_{tot}.

$$y_{tot}(age) = y1(age) + y_{r>1}(age). \tag{6}$$

The appendix to MacLeod et al. 2012, (pp. 212–217, 227–229) describes the mathematical foundation for the theory and the estimation procedures used both for the individual parameters of the models and for the number of offenders allocated to each category.

2.4 Conclusions

In conclusion, this section has described a simple quantitative theory of criminal careers that specifies that offenders can be divided into three categories based on their risk of reconviction and their rate of offending: *HH*, *HL*, and *LL*. In MacLeod et al. 2012, this quantitative model was shown to fit various OI data sets very well. The parameters are meaningful, and the important age–crime curve is closely fitted, as is the number of convictions of each individual. The remainder of this Element investigates how well this model, and associated theory, fits criminal career data from the CSDD and PYS.

3 Application to the Cambridge Study in Delinquent Development (CSDD)

3.1 The CSDD

The CSDD is a prospective longitudinal survey of 411 London males who were first studied in 1961–1962 at age 8–9. Their parents, teachers, peers, female partners, and children have also been interviewed. At the time they were first contacted in 1961–1962, the males were all living in a working-class area of South London. The vast majority of the sample was chosen by taking all the males who were then aged 8–9 and on the registers of six state primary schools within a one-mile radius of a research office, which had been established. In addition to 399 males from these six schools, 12 males from a local school for 'educationally subnormal' (special needs) children were included in the sample, in an attempt to make it more representative of the population of males living in the area. Therefore, the males were not a probability sample drawn from a population, but rather a complete population of males of that age in that area at that time. The males have been interviewed or assessed nine times, at ages 8, 10, 14, 16, 18, 21, 25, 32, and 48.

Most of the males (357, or 87 per cent) were White in appearance and of British origin, in the sense that they were being brought up by parents who had themselves been brought up in England, Scotland, or Wales. Of the remaining 54 males, 12 were African-Caribbean, having at least one parent of West Indian (usually) or African origin. Of the remaining 42 males of non-British origin, 14 had at least one parent from the North or South of Ireland; 12 had parents from Cyprus; and the other 16 males were White and had at least one parent from another Western industrialized country.

On the basis of their fathers' occupations when they were aged 8, 94 per cent of the males could be described as working-class (categories III, IV, or V on the Registrar General's scale, describing skilled, semi-skilled, or unskilled manual workers, respectively), in comparison with the national figure of 78 per cent at that time. The majority of the males were living in conventional two-parent families with both a father and a mother figure; at age 8, only 6 per cent of the males had no operative father, and only 1 per cent had no operative mother. This was, therefore, overwhelmingly a traditional White, urban, working-class sample of British origin.

The results of the CSDD have been described in six books (Farrington et al., 2013; Piquero et al., 2007; West, 1969, 1982; West & Farrington, 1973, 1977) and in eight summary articles (Farrington, 1995, 2003, 2019, 2021; Farrington & West, 1981, 1990; Farrington et al., 2009, 2021).

The CSDD males were followed up in criminal records from age 10 to age 61 at the last sweep.[7] Of the cohort, 7 emigrated prior to age 21, none of whom were convicted in the UK; 44 have died up to age 61 (19 before and 25 after age 50); and 177 of the cohort individuals sustained one or more criminal convictions, with a total of 860 court appearances. Of the convicted men, 4 appear to have permanently emigrated up to age 48, and 31 have died up to age 61 (13 before and 18 after age 50). The impact of emigration and death is discussed where appropriate. In the analysis that follows, each court appearance is counted as only one conviction, depending on the principal offence.

3.2 CSDD *Risk* Analysis

We start the analysis of the CSDD data by creating conviction records for each court appearance containing date of birth, date of conviction, date of offence, conviction number, inter-conviction time, and court disposal. Table 1 lists the total number of offenders with each conviction number. The data are plotted in Figure 3 (+ symbol on the graph) using a logarithmic *y*-axis, in keeping with the MacLeod et al. analysis described in Section 2.

Following the procedures outlined in MacLeod et al. 2012 and described in Section 2, the 'dual-*risk* recidivism model' (Eq. (1)) was fitted to the data. The parameter values are listed in Table 2, and the results are plotted in Figure 3. The solid line is a plot of the fitted model. The *low-risk* component of the model and the *low-risk* residuals[8] are plotted separately (shown as dotted line and square symbols, respectively), to highlight the influence of the *low-risk* category offenders. In this much smaller data set, the *low-risk* residuals disappear after only two convictions. The estimated dual-*risk* model fitted the CSDD data extremely well, and over 99 per cent of the variance in the data of Table 1 was explained by the model. However, the parameter values (Table 2) differ from those estimated for male offenders in the OI 1953 cohort (MacLeod et al. 2012, p. 41). After due consideration, it was thought unlikely that death or emigration would have had any significant impact on the recidivism *risk* analysis.

The majority of men in the CSDD were born in 1953 and should therefore be directly comparable with the OI 1953 cohort males. However, they were all from an inner-city working-class part of London and hence were a demographically selected *high-risk* sample. This is a possible explanation for the much higher proportion of the CSDD offenders in the *high-risk* category, 0.733 as opposed to 0.269 for the OI 1953 cohort males. The *high-risk* probability p_1 is the same in

---

[7] None of the emigrants was followed up outside the UK after age 32.

[8] The *low-risk* residuals are calculated as the difference between the data and the *high-risk* component of the model, that is, the *high-risk* component is the straight line between n = 5 and n = 25 projected backwards to n = 1 in Figure 3.

Table 1 Count (*N*) of offenders with *n* or more principal convictions in the CSDD

Conviction no. (*n*)	1	2	3	4	5	6	7	8	9	10
Count *N*	177	123	91	73	65	54	40	36	32	28
Conviction no. (*n*)	11	12	13	14	15	16	17	18	19	20
Count *N*	24	19	16	15	14	12	9	6	4	2
Conviction no. (*n*)	21	22	23	24	25	26	27	28	29	30
Count *N*	2	2	2	2	2	2	2	2	2	2

Table 2 Parameter values for the dual-*risk* model

Data	Cohort prevalence	*A*	*a*	*p₁*	*p₂*	Variance explained
CSDD	43%	177	0.73	0.84	0.24	99.8%
OI 1953 cohort	37%	9399	0.27	0.84	0.35	99.9%

Notes: A = number of first convictions, a = proportion of *high-risk* offenders, p_1 = *high-risk* probability of reconviction, and p_2 = *low-risk* probability of reconviction

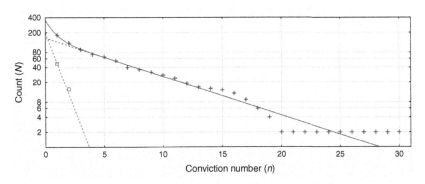

Figure 3 Count (*N*) of offenders with *n* or more convictions versus conviction number (*n*) in the CSDD

both cohorts at 0.84. Interestingly the *low-risk* parameter p_2 is significantly lower in the CSDD cohort at 0.24, compared with 0.35 in the OI. This difference could suggest that some of the potential *low-risk* offenders might have been recruited into the *high-risk* category because of the higher prevalence of criminal activity within peer groups, leaving behind a smaller and less criminal *low-risk* category. In addition, the overall prevalence of criminality at 43 per cent is also higher than in the 1953 birth cohort at 37 per cent (MacLeod et al. 2012, p. 41).

3.3 CSDD *Rate* Analysis

The dual-*rate* survival model (Eq. (2)) was fitted to the CSDD inter-conviction
survival time data, which again resulted in an excellent fit, with over 99 per cent
of the variance in the data accounted for. However, the data diverges from the
theoretical curve for inter-conviction survival times greater than twenty years.
Death and emigration are potential causes of this divergence. From the data, it is
possible to estimate, for each individual, given the number of previous convictions, the probability of reconviction and the probability of conviction beyond the
date of death or emigration, given the date of the last conviction. The product of
these probabilities gives the probability that that individual might have been
reconvicted if he had not died or emigrated. The sum of these probabilities,
over all deceased and emigrants, with previous convictions, provides an estimate
of the number of 'false survivals': for the CSDD cohort, this sum equals 2.99.
Adding this number to Eq. (2) and refitting to the data provide a marginal
improvement to the fit but considerable support for the argument that death and
emigration may be the cause of the divergence seen in Figure 4. The survival data
(shown as o symbols on the graph) and fitted curves are plotted in Figure 4. The
dotted line is the fitted curve for Eq. (2), and the solid line is the fitted curve with
2.99 added to Eq 2.2; the solid line now agrees very well with the data points.

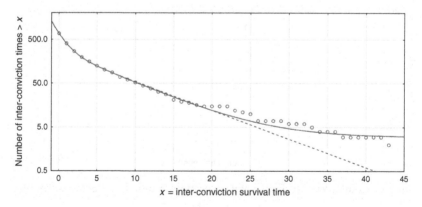

Figure 4 Number of inter-conviction times[9] >x in the CSDD

Table 3 lists the parameter estimates for the CSDD and OI cohorts. The CSDD
parameter values are for the modified Eq. (2) fit. Comparing the CSDD parameter estimates with the OI 1953 cohort values reveals some differences between
the two. In the CSDD cohort, λ_2 (the *low-rate* convictions per year) is slightly

---

[9] Individual recidivists with more than two convictions contribute several inter-conviction times to
the count on the y-axis.

Table 3 Comparison of parameter estimates for the
dual-*rate* survival model

Cohort	b	λ_1	λ_2
CSDD	0.61	0.87	0.17
53 OI cohort males	0.56	0.85	0.21

Notes: b = the proportion of *high-rate* reconviction times,
λ_1 = number of *high-rate* reconvictions per year, and λ_2 = number
of *low-rate* reconvictions per year

lower (longer reconviction times) than in the OI cohort, with λ_2 at 0.17 in the
CSDD cohort and 0.21 in the OI cohort. Remarkably, λ_1 is essentially the same in
both cohorts at 0.87 and 0.85, respectively. The proportion of those with *high
rate* in the CSDD cohort is slightly higher than in the OI cohort at 0.61 and 0.56,
respectively. The longer reconviction times again suggest a possible recruitment
effect of *low-rate* category offenders into the more criminally active group due to
peer influence and a higher overall prevalence of criminal behaviour.

3.4 Theoretical Offender Category Allocation

Applying the allocation procedures outlined in the appendix to MacLeod et al.
2012, (pp. 215–217), the number and proportion of offenders in each *risk/rate*
category were calculated, and these are shown in Table 4. The proportion of *HH*
offenders in the CSDD cohort is over twice that of the whole population sample
from the OI, reflecting the higher criminality in inner-city working-class samples. The higher proportion of *LL* offenders in the OI sample reflects the
inclusion of urban and rural areas with a higher proportion of white-collar
/professional populations in that sample.

Table 4 Allocation of offenders to the *risk/rate* categories

	CSDD				OI 1953 males			
	High-risk		*Low-risk*		*High-risk*		*Low-risk*	
High-rate	81	46%	–	–	339	19%	–	–
Low-rate	48	27%	48	27%	609	8%	5,558	73%
Total	129	73%	48	27%	948	27%	5,558	73%

3.5 Age–Conviction Analysis

Table 5 lists the number of 'first' and 'all' convictions at each age for the CSDD
cohort. It can be seen that the peak age for first convictions was at 14–15,
whereas the peak age for all convictions was at 17–18. There were no first

Table 5 Age profile for convictions in the CSDD

Age	10	11	12	13	14	15	16	17	18	19	20	21	22
First conviction	8	7	7	13	21	23	14	15	10	6	9	3	4
All convictions	9	11	12	24	47	55	51	58	60	45	43	32	34

Age	23	24	25	26	27	28	29	30	31	32	33	34	35
First conviction	1	2	4	3	1	1	1	1	2	4	0	4	2
All convictions	15	14	21	21	16	14	17	18	12	14	11	13	16

Age	36	37	38	39	40	41	42	43	44	45	46	47	48
First conviction	0	0	1	1	1	0	0	0	1	1	0	1	1
All convictions	8	12	6	4	9	9	8	13	16	9	8	4	8

Age	49	50	51	52	53	54	55	56	57	58	59	60	61
First conviction	2	0	1	1	0	0	0	0	0	0	0	0	0
All convictions	7	7	8	2	4	3	5	6	5	4	4	3	5

convictions after age 52, but reconvictions continued to occur up to age 61. The probability that any of the emigrants or deceased would have been convicted for the first time after emigration or death was estimated at less than 0.02, and it has, therefore, not been considered in the age at first conviction analysis.

The complete survival model for first convictions (Eq. (3)) was estimated using the *rate* parameters from Table 3 and the proportion *high rate* from Table 4. The results are shown in Table 6. The fitted curve and data for the CSDD are plotted in Figure 5 (with a logarithmic *y*-axis).

The fit of the survival model to the CSDD cohort data is again very good, with 99 per cent of variance accounted for. There were no first convictions after age 52, but the three individuals who were convicted at ages 50, 51, and 52 would appear to have been convicted a little earlier than predicted by the theory. The parameter estimates are broadly consistent with the OI 1953 cohort values, but the parameter (*a*), at 0.97 for the CSDD rather than 0.54 for the OI, results in a steeper rise in convictions during the teenage years, and *c* at 13.49 rather than 14.68 results in the steepest increase a year earlier than in the OI 1953 cohort males, which results in an earlier peak in the age at both first and all conviction curves.

Table 6 Parameter estimates for survival to
first conviction model

	CSDD	**OI 1953 males**
α	0.96	0.54
c	13.5	14.7
P_f	0.55	0.51

Notes: α = slope of the rise in crime transition, c = midpoint age of the rise in crime transition, and P_f = relative probability of a first conviction

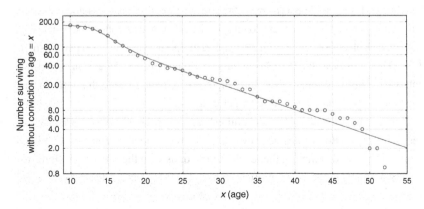

Figure 5 Survival to first conviction curve for the CSDD

Criminology

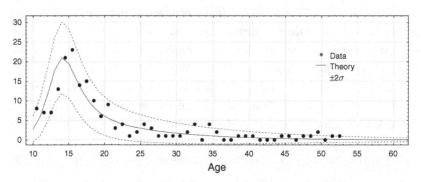

Figure 6 Number of first convictions versus age in the CSDD

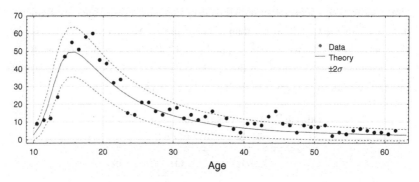

Figure 7 Number of all convictions versus age in the CSDD

Substituting the parameter values listed in Tables 3 and 6 in Eq. (4) and using the category allocation proportions in Table 4, the expected number of first convictions was calculated for both *high-* and *low-rate* offenders at each age. These were summed, giving the theoretical age at first conviction curve, shown as the continuous line in Figure 6. The $\pm 2\sigma$ ($\sigma \equiv$ standard deviation) bounds assume a Poisson distribution about the theoretical count at each age (shown as dotted lines). The data is plotted as black dot symbols on the graph. The age at first conviction data from the CSDD lies mostly within the $\pm 2\sigma$ bounds (approximately the 95 per cent confidence interval), with only three of the forty-eight points lying outside this interval (i.e. 6 per cent rather than the expected 5 per cent).

Solving the differential Eq. (6), numerically, for each of the *risk/rate* categories, with parameter values as previously given and reconviction probabilities from Table 2, and summing the reconviction totals with the first convictions, for each age point, yield the theoretical age–conviction curve, shown as the solid line in Figure 7. As before, the data is plotted as dot symbols, and the $\pm 2\sigma$

bounds are shown as dotted lines. Again, most data points lie within the $\pm 2\sigma$ error bounds with only five points lying outside. The analysis takes no account of time spent in custody, which could account for lower counts in the mid-twenties and delayed convictions later in the career.

3.6 Conclusions

The *risk/rate* model, described in Section 2 and developed for the OI cohort, fitted the CSDD criminal career data very well: the number of males with n or more convictions, time intervals between convictions, the age–crime curve, and the age at first conviction curve. Remarkably, the *risk* of recidivism, of the *high-risk* category, and the *rate* of offending, of the *high-rate* category, were the same in both cohorts. The *risk* of recidivism, of the *low-risk* category, and the *rate* of offending, of the *low-rate* category, were slightly lower in the CSDD than in the OI, possibly because of the higher prevalence of *high-risk* offenders in the CSDD cohort. The next section investigates the extent to which the CSDD offenders in different *risk/rate* categories could be predicted by childhood risk factors.

4 Childhood Prediction of *Risk/Rate* Categories in the CSDD

The MacLeod et al. theory, outlined in Section 2, was inspired by models developed using data from the UK OI. The models (Eqs. (1) and (2)) were successfully applied to the CSDD cohort data in Section 3. With allowances made for the demographic and data collection differences in the different cohorts, the estimated parameters of the models were found to be remarkably similar between the cohorts. In addition to the criminal career information analysed in Section 3, the CSDD collected a great deal of information on the personal circumstances of the cohort members. In this section, the data collected in childhood in the CSDD is related to the *risk/rate* categories discovered in Section 3. The key issue is whether different explanatory risk factors predict the different *risk/rate* categories.

4.1 Allocating Cases to *Risk/Rate* Categories

The modelling has identified three theoretical offender categories, *HH*,[10] *HL*, and *LL*. The models provide estimates of the numbers of individuals in

---

[10] Theoretical categories in italics (*HH*, *HL*, and *LL*). Data derived categories in the roman text (HH, HL, and LL).

each of these *risk/rate* categories but do not identify which individuals belong to which category. From the data, we can determine, for each individual, both the number of convictions and the mean inter-conviction time (or alternatively the annual rate of conviction), and by choosing suitable cut-off points, individuals can be allocated to data-derived *risk/rate* categories (HH, HL, and LL).

Table 4 shows the theoretical allocation of individuals to the theoretical offender categories, in which 81 are *HH*, 48 are *HL* (a total of 129 *high-risk*), and 48 are *LL* and *low-risk*. Selecting a cut-off point of 2 or more convictions to identify *high-risk* individuals and an average conviction rate greater than 0.283 convictions per year as *high-rate*, 81 offenders are designated HH, 42 as HL (a total of 123 *high-risk*) and 54 as LL and *low-risk*.

From Section 3, the theory predicts that 21 ($129 * (1 - p_1)$) actual *high-risk* individuals would have only 1 conviction and would be designated *low-risk* by the cut-off, while 12 ($42 * p_2$) actual *low-risk* individuals would have 2 or more convictions and be designated *high-risk* by the cut-off. While the theory predicted that the cut-off would identify 120 as *high-risk* and 57 as *low-risk*, 123 *high-risk* were found, in the data, by the cut-off. It is unlikely that any of the misallocated *risk* categories would have been *high-rate*. Therefore, the misallocation is probably confined to the *low-rate* offenders, accounting for the slight excess in the LL and the shortfall in the HL categories, in the cut-off points-based allocation. There is clearly some overlap in the allocations, but in the main, the categories would appear to be accurately identified and can be associated with individuals (see Table 7).

Table 7 Numerical comparison of theoretical allocations (Table 4) with data-derived cut-off-based allocations

	LL	*HL*	*HH*
Theoretical allocations	48	48	81
Data cut-off-based allocations	54	42	81

A serious shortcoming of the MacLeod et al. analysis was that the personal characteristics of individuals were only available using data from the OASys;[11]

---

[11] The OASys was developed by and is used by the prison and probation services of England and Wales.

only offenders in the care of the prison or probation service were assessed, and that assessment was contemporary rather than prospective. Although this personal information is useful in predicting the future offending of serious offenders, it sheds no light on the potential criminal careers of those reaching the age of criminal responsibility (10 in England and Wales). In section 4.2, this issue is addressed using individual behavioural and environmental risk factor assessment data, measured at age 8–10, for 409 boys in the CSDD (i.e. excluding the 2 boys who emigrated prior to age 10).

4.2 Childhood Risk Factors

At age 8–10 in the CSDD, the aim was to measure as many variables as possible that were believed (at the time) to predict delinquency. There was a concern that too many criminological studies measured and analysed a very limited number of variables. In many CSDD analyses, the age 8–10 variables were dichotomized into the 'worst' quarter versus the remainder. This facilitated a risk factor approach, made all the risk factors comparable, and did not usually involve much loss of information, as many variables were originally measured on 2, 3, or 4 point scales (Farrington & Loeber, 2000). They were not measured on normally distributed equal-interval scales.

The CSDD risk factors that are studied in this Element comprised twenty-five of the thirty important risk factors studied by Farrington (2020b). A convicted mother was excluded because of its rarity; only 7 per cent of the boys had convicted mothers, whereas around a quarter of the boys were in the risk category of all other variables. Low parental interest in children, authoritarian parents, an uninvolved father, and high dishonesty were excluded because these risk factors were not known for more than 10 per cent of the boys. The remaining twenty-five risk factors are as follows:

Parental: Father convicted prior to age 32 (when almost all of the boys were below age 10) was obtained from criminal record searches. Most other parental and family factors were based on ratings by the psychiatric social workers who interviewed the boys' parents. Young fathers were those who had their first child before age 23, while young mothers were those who had their first child before age 21. Low parental interest in the boy's education was rated by the psychiatric social workers. The rating of a depressed mother was also based on these interviews, but it also took account of information about psychiatric treatment and scores on a mother's health questionnaire.

Family: Harsh attitude and discipline were based on psychiatric social worker assessments of both parents, as was poor parental supervision, which referred to the extent to which the parents knew what the boy was doing when he was outside the house. Parental conflict was also rated by the psychiatric social workers based on their interviews with the parents, and it referred to chronic tensions or disagreement in many fields, raging conflicts, or estrangement. A disrupted family referred to the temporary or permanent separation of a boy from a parent before the boy's tenth birthday for reasons other than death or hospitalization.

Socio-economic: Poor housing (very dilapidated) and low family income were rated by the psychiatric social workers. Large family size referred to five or more children born to the boy's mother up to his tenth birthday. Low socio-economic status referred to fathers who had unskilled manual jobs. Information about high-delinquency-rate schools was obtained from the local education authority.

Attainment: Low non-verbal IQ of the boy was measured by the Progressive Matrices test, while low verbal IQ was based on verbal comprehension and vocabulary tests. Low junior school attainment of the boy was based on school records of arithmetic, English, and verbal reasoning tests completed by the boys.

Personality: High daring was rated by parents and peers, and identified boys who took many risks in traffic, climbing, exploring, and so on. High hyperactivity was based on ratings by teachers of whether the boy lacked concentration or was restless in class. High impulsivity was based on psychomotor tests of clumsiness. High neuroticism and extraversion were based on scores on the New Junior Maudsley Inventory (Gibson, 1967) that was completed by the boys. Low popularity was based on peer ratings.

Behaviour: High troublesomeness was rated by peers and teachers, identifying boys who got into trouble most. Difficult to discipline was rated by teachers.

4.3 Risk Factors Predicting *Risk/Rate* Categories

Table 8 shows the odds ratio (OR) for the individuals' allocation to the corresponding category (HH, HL, or LL), all compared with not-convicted (NC) individuals, together with the proportion allocated without (NR) and with (R) the corresponding risk factor, and the significance of the OR. For example, in studying convicted fathers, 81 HH males were compared with 227 NC males. Of 53 with convicted fathers, 31 (58.5 per cent) were in the HH category, compared with 50 out of 255 (19.6 per cent) who had unconvicted fathers (OR = 5.78; $p < 0.0001$; the one-tailed test was used because of directional predictions).

Table 8 CSDD age 8–10 risk factors predicting *risk/rate* categories

	HH			HL			LL		
	% R	% NR	OR	% R	% NR	OR	% R	% NR	OR
Parental									
Convicted father	58.5	19.6	5.78**	35.3	12.8	3.73**	40.5	15.6	3.68**
Young father	20.4	27.4	0.68	20.4	14.1	1.56	20.4	18.3	1.14
Young mother	25.6	26.6	0.95	25.6	10.9	2.80**	20.0	17.7	1.16
Low interest in education	46.2	20.6	3.30**	24.3	14.4	1.92	6.7	20.3	0.28*
Depressed mother	34.8	20.3	2.09**	20.0	13.7	1.57	21.1	17.8	1.23
Family									
Harsh discipline	36.5	20.7	2.20**	23.9	12.2	2.26**	15.6	19.5	0.76
Poor supervision	44.7	21.0	3.04**	38.1	11.3	4.82**	25.7	17.9	1.59
Parental conflict	43.9	18.3	3.50**	26.0	11.7	2.66**	19.6	19.1	1.03
Disrupted family	43.9	22.3	2.72**	36.0	11.0	4.57**	30.4	16.7	2.19**
Socio-economic									
Poor housing	39.4	19.6	2.67**	25.0	11.4	2.60**	28.4	14.6	2.32**
Low family income	45.1	20.7	3.15**	25.0	13.4	2.16**	18.8	19.0	0.99
Large family size	46.4	20.5	3.35**	32.7	11.2	3.85**	21.3	18.5	1.19
Low SES	37.7	23.5	1.97**	17.4	15.2	1.17	20.8	18.5	1.16

Table 8 (cont.)

	HH			HL			LL		
	% R	% NR	OR	% R	% NR	OR	% R	% NR	OR
High delinquency school	49.1	22.3	3.37**	30.0	13.6	2.71**	26.3	19.0	1.53
Attainment									
Low non-verbal IQ	44.0	20.6	3.03**	23.6	13.6	1.97*	25.0	17.4	1.58
Low verbal IQ	40.3	21.9	2.41**	25.9	12.9	2.35**	23.2	18.0	1.38
Low attainment	50.0	20.1	3.98**	28.9	11.6	3.10**	28.9	16.4	2.07*
Personality									
High daring	48.3	17.9	4.28**	27.4	12.3	2.70**	25.0	17.5	1.57
High impulsivity	40.5	21.8	2.45**	21.4	14.1	1.66	27.9	16.4	1.96**
High hyperactivity	45.8	21.7	3.05**	17.9	14.8	1.25	31.9	16.3	2.41**
High neuroticism	31.0	22.8	1.52	20.5	13.1	1.72	20.5	17.4	1.23
High extraversion	28.7	23.6	1.31	19.5	13.4	1.57	16.2	19.0	0.83
Low popularity	29.7	23.9	1.34	22.0	11.7	2.13**	20.0	17.2	1.20
Behaviour									
High troublesomeness	54.7	18.9	5.19**	31.0	12.8	3.06**	31.0	16.8	2.22**
Difficult to discipline	47.6	20.8	3.46**	26.7	13.0	2.43**	32.7	16.0	2.54**

Note: The OR significance level is based on 2x2 cross tabulation of risk factor versus *risk/rate* category, X^2 test with * = $p < 0.1$ and ** = $p < 0.05$ as indicated.

The strongest predictors of HH males were a convicted father (OR = 5.78), high troublesomeness (OR = 5.19), high daring (OR = 4.28), low attainment (OR = 3.98), parental conflict (OR = 3.50), and difficult to discipline (OR = 3.46). The strongest predictors of HL males were poor parental supervision (OR = 4.82), a disrupted family (OR = 4.57), large family size (OR = 3.85), a convicted father (OR = 3.73), low attainment (OR = 3.10), and high troublesomeness (OR = 3.06). It can be seen that the four strongest predictors of HL were not among the strongest predictors of HH males.

Not surprisingly there were fewer significant or near-significant ($p < 0.1$) predictors of LL males (only 10) than of HH (20) or HL males (16). Furthermore, one of the significant predictors of LL males was in the 'wrong' direction; low parental interest in education predicted a low probability of being an LL male. Excluding this puzzling result, the strongest predictors of LL males were a convicted father (OR = 3.92), difficult to discipline (OR = 2.48), high hyperactivity (OR = 2.34), a disrupted family (OR = 2.34), poor housing (OR = 2.24), and high troublesomeness (OR = 2.16). Three of these overlapped with the six strongest predictors of HH males, and three overlapped with the six strongest predictors of HL males.

4.4 Logistic Regression Analyses

For each of the *risk/rate* categories (HH, HL, and LL), the significant risk factors from Table 8 were selected and used in forward stepwise logistic regression analyses to investigate which risk factors predicted the *risk/rate* categories, compared to NC males, independently of other risk factors. It is important to investigate independent predictors because, of course, some of the risk factors are significantly related to other risk factors (especially to those in the same category). For example, low family income was significantly related to large family size (OR = 9.7), high-delinquency-rate school (OR = 5.3) and poor housing (OR = 4.8), and low verbal IQ was significantly related to low school attainment (OR = 10.7) and low non-verbal IQ (OR = 6.1).

Because of our interest in identifying explanatory risk factors, the behavioural risk factors (high troublesomeness and difficult to discipline) were excluded from these analyses. It seems likely that these risk factors may be measuring the same underlying construct as offending (e.g. a criminal or antisocial personality); therefore, the fact that they predict offending probably does not reflect any kind of causal effect on offending but merely the persistence of this underlying construct.

First, we entered all the significant predictors in a forward stepwise logistic regression to see which ones came out as significant (or near-significant) independent predictors. The only exception was that we did not enter low interest in education in predicting *low-risk/low-rate* offenders because this risk factor was (counter-intuitively) negatively related to offending (at only $p = 0.07$). After this first analysis, we continued entering significant (and near-significant) predictors from each regression in further regressions until the final model was clear.

Table 9 shows the results of the logistic regression analyses. The strongest independent predictors of the HH category were a convicted father, high daring, low attainment, a disrupted family, poor housing, and low non-verbal IQ. The strongest five of the six predictors were drawn from five different risk factor categories: parental, family, socio-economic, attainment, and personality. These results are quite typical of results obtained in the CSDD for the prediction of offending in general. Typically, about five risk factors from five different categories are found to be independent predictors of convictions. For example, Farrington et al. (2009) studied the age 8–10 predictors of convictions up to age 50. The strongest independent predictors were a convicted parent, high daring, low attainment, poor housing, and a disrupted family – remarkably similar to the strongest independent predictors of the HH category.

The strongest predictors of the HL category were somewhat different. Poor supervision and large family size were the strongest independent predictors, followed by a disrupted family, low attainment, and poor housing. These predictors were drawn from only three categories: family, socio-economic, and attainment. While parental (a convicted father) and personality (high daring) factors were the strongest independent predictors of the HH category, they were not among the significant independent predictors of the HL category.

The strongest predictors of the LL category were a convicted father and poor housing. A disrupted family was the next most important (near-significant) factor. Again, these predictors were drawn from only three categories: parental, family, and socio-economic. Attainment and personality factors were not important predictors of the LL category.

4.5 Identifying *Risk/Rate* Categories from the Risk Factors

The logistic regression identified three sets of risk factors associated with the retrospectively determined *risk/rate* categories, HH, HL, and LL. The factors identified by the regressions are those that significantly increase the odds of an individual with those risk factors belonging to the category in question. By coding the identified factors (*risk* = 1 and no *risk* = 0) and summing over the significant risk factors for each category (Table 9), a category factor score can be generated for each individual, which is related to the likelihood of that

Table 9 Results of logistic regression analyses

	LRCS	*P*	POR	*P*
High-risk/high-rate (*N* = 290)				
Convicted father	28.03	0.0001	2.81	0.003
High daring	20.19	0.0001	3.94	0.0001
Low attainment	17.10	0.0001	3.40	0.0004
Disrupted family	5.95	0.007	2.46	0.010
Poor housing	4.69	0.015	1.97	0.017
Low non-verbal IQ	3.54	0.030	1.96	0.029
High-risk/low-rate (*N* = 237)				
Poor supervision	15.74	0.0001	3.17	0.006
Large family size	8.65	0.002	2.60	0.015
Disrupted family	6.03	0.007	2.60	0.016
Low attainment	2.70	0.050	2.12	0.053
Poor housing	1.71	0.095	1.75	0.093
Low-risk/low-rate (*N* = 281)				
Convicted father	12.55	0.0002	2.96	0.003
Poor housing	3.57	0.029	1.82	0.033
Disrupted family	1.65	0.099	1.65	0.095

Notes: LRCS = likelihood ratio chi-squared improvement, POR = partial odds ratio, and one-tailed *p* values

individual being a member of the respective category. As an example, for the LL factor score, a boy with a convicted father and poor housing but not a disrupted family would have a score of 2. For the scores to be meaningful for individuals, cases with missing risk factors, for that category factor score, were omitted from the analyses.

The scores provide a ranking of the individuals with respect to each category, which facilitated a receiver operating characteristic (ROC) analysis to be carried out. The logistic regressions described previously compared each of the data-derived categories (HH, HL, and LL) with NC, and the results of the ROC analyses for these subsets of the data are shown in Figure 8. The area under the ROC curve (AUC) is the probability that any two cases, chosen at random, would be ranked correctly by the score and is a measure of how well the score discriminates. With AUCs of 0.72, 0.64, and 0.64, the HH, HL, and LL categories are correctly identified with corresponding probabilities. However, this level of identification is achieved on subsets of the data, including only the

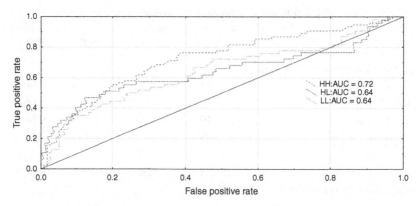

Figure 8 ROC curves for HH versus NC, HL versus NC, and LL versus NC

category in question versus NC, and the categories have been retrospectively determined.

Perfect prediction would not be expected because the probabilistic theory would specify that a certain fraction of true *HH* males would actually be identified as HL or LL males (and a corresponding statement would apply to true *HL* and *LL* males). If, in reality, the categories correspond to groups of individuals with similar risk factors then, for a prospectively predicted group of size Ng, the theory predicts that $Ng * p$ would be convicted in their lifetime, $Ng * (1-p)$ would remain unconvicted, $Ng * (p - p^2)$ would have just one conviction, $Ng * (p^2 - p^3)$ would have just two convictions, and so on. Similarly, the proportion with zero or one conviction would have no inter-conviction times; those with two or more convictions with exponentially distributed inter-conviction times could have both short and long intervals. Any dichotomies chosen for retrospective allocation to categories will inevitably lead to some misallocation.

Figure 9 shows the prospective probability of category membership versus category factor scores for each of the scores (HH score, HL score, and LL score). Valid category factor scores were calculated for 377, 352, and 404 cohort members for HH, HL, and LL scores respectively. The graphs in Figure 9 show category factor scores (the sum of significant risk factors for each category, see Table 9) on the bottom *x*-axis, number of individuals (*n*) with that score on the top *x*-axis, and probability of individuals with that score retrospectively being allocated to the HH, HL, and LL, categories or NC, on the *y*-axis. The solid lines indicate the retrospectively allocated category, related to the score on the bottom *x*-axis.

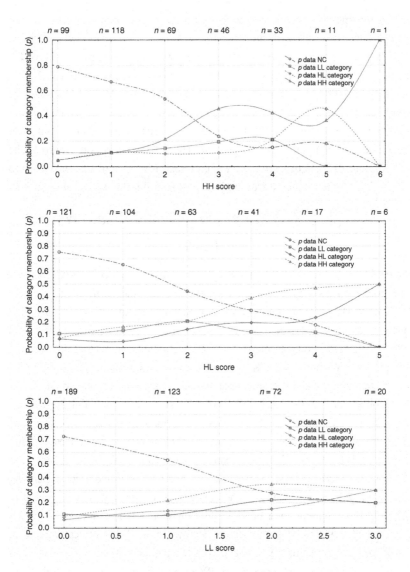

Figure 9 Probability of retrospective-category membership for each category factor score

4.6 Conclusions

These analyses show the extent to which the HH, HL, and LL categories can be predicted from childhood (age 8–10) risk factors in the CSDD. This is a step towards expanding our simple theory (which predicts criminal career features) into a more complex theory that specifies the influence of risk factors. Prediction scores were calculated for each of the risk/rate categories. In general, each of the analyses shows an increasing probability of membership of one of the risk/rate categories with increasing scores. However, there is considerable overlap in the independently significant predictors. All three predictors of LL are also among the six predictors of HH, and two are also predictors of HL. It is therefore not surprising that the LL score also predicts HH and HL category membership. It is also interesting to note that low intelligence and high daring are uniquely predictors of the HH category, while large families and poor supervision are uniquely predictors of the HL category. Section 5 derives the *HH*, *HL*, and *LL* categories in the PYS, and Section 6 investigates the extent to which they can be predicted from risk factors in childhood and adolescence.

5 Application to the Pittsburgh Youth Study (PYS)

5.1 The PYS

The PYS started data collection in 1987–1988, with three age cohorts of inner-city boys from the Pittsburgh Public School system. The principal investigators were Rolf Loeber, David P. Farrington, and Magda Stouthamer-Loeber. David Farrington continued as a co–principal investigator of the PYS for about thirty years, from 1986 to 2015. The youngest cohort ($N = 503$), the middle cohort ($N = 508$), and the oldest cohort ($N = 506$) were assessed first every six months and later (only in the case of the youngest and oldest cohorts) annually. Because only the youngest and oldest cohorts were continuously followed up, most analyses (including those in this Element) are only based on these cohorts. Information was collected from the males, their parents, and their teachers. The PYS is one of the longest-running longitudinal studies on delinquency and mental health in the United States. The PYS has generated numerous books, chapters, and peer-reviewed articles spanning a large number of different outcomes including delinquency, serious violence, mental health problems, and other health behaviours. The main books are by Loeber et al. (1998, 2008), Loeber and Farrington (2011), and Jennings et al. (2016), and a recent summary article is by Ahonen et al. (2021).

Since one of the main purposes of the PYS was to investigate serious offending, an initial screener was used to identify particularly high-risk participants. Out of approximately 1,000 boys who were identified for each cohort, about 850 boys in each cohort were screened using the self-reported antisocial behaviour (SRA) scale for the youngest and middle cohorts. This instrument was developed by Loeber et al. (1989). The youngest cohort was aged about 7 at baseline, and the SRA was considered to be more age-appropriate than the self-reported delinquency (SRD) scale at this point in development. The oldest cohort (average age 13) was screened using the SRD (adjusted from the national youth survey instrument by Loeber et al. 1998). Parents and teachers added information to the screening process through responding to the child behaviour checklist (CBCL).

Out of approximately 850 boys who were screened in each cohort, about 250 were chosen for follow-up based on being classified as high-risk, and about 250 were chosen at random from the remaining 600. The three age cohorts were similar on most demographic variables. The youngest cohort was assessed at least annually from age 7 to age 19, while the oldest cohort was assessed at least annually from age 13 to age 25. Participation rates were high; for example, 82 per cent of the youngest cohort were still assessed at age 19, and 83 per cent of the oldest cohort were still assessed at age 25. The middle cohort was only assessed regularly from age 10 to age 13. As mentioned, only the youngest and oldest cohorts are studied in this Element, as in the book by Loeber et al. (2008).

Many different variables were measured in the PYS. The primary constructs were categorized as child, family, and other factors. The child constructs were delinquency, substance use, psychopathology and conduct problems, sexual behaviour, injuries, attitudes, and competence. The family factors included discipline, supervision, involvement, positive parenting, communication, attitudes, relationships, parent stress, and parent psychopathology. In the category called 'other', the following constructs were assessed: peer delinquency, peer substance use, prosocial peers/friends, demographic/socio-economic factors, and neighborhood. In addition, criminal record searches were carried out up to 2012 when the youngest cohort were aged about 32 and the oldest cohort were aged about 38 (see Ahonen et al., 2020; Loeber et al., 2017; Theobald et al., 2014). The convictions data set shows the number of offences of each offender at each age. The data specify all charges leading to convictions, so one criminal event could result in several convictions (Jennings et al., 2016).

5.2 PYS *Risk* Analysis

In this study, conviction records for the PYS cohorts were created for each conviction containing: ID, conviction number, age (integer years) at conviction, offence type, and inter-conviction time (age difference from previous conviction). Multiple convictions at the same age were counted as separate convictions but generated zero inter-conviction times, and convictions were numbered 1 for the first conviction, 2 for the second, and so on. Table 10 shows the frequency of conviction numbers, for the youngest and oldest cohorts.

The entry under conviction no. 1 shows the number of individuals in each cohort with 1 or more convictions within the follow-up period. Of the 503 males in the youngest cohort, 196 were convicted (39 per cent), and 1 male had 33 convictions. Of the 506 males in the oldest cohort, 235 (46 per cent) were convicted, and 1 male had 42 convictions. The difference in the number of males convicted is, in part, explained by the absence of late-onset offenders in

Table 10 Count (N) of offenders with n or more convictions

Conviction no. (n)	1	2	3	4	5	6	7	8	9	10	11	12	13	14	15	16	17	18
Youngest con count (N)	196	141	111	90	71	50	37	34	29	26	21	19	15	13	10	8	5	4
Oldest con count (N)	235	181	150	122	97	75	61	52	46	41	37	31	26	21	19	16	15	14
Conviction no. (n)	19	20	21	22	23	24	25	26	27	28	29	30	31	32	33	34	…	42
Youngest con count (N)	3	2	2	2	2	2	2	1	1	1	1	1	1	1	1	1	…	1
Oldest con count (N)	12	12	12	10	8	5	5	4	4	3	3	1	1	1	1	1	…	1

the youngest cohort, estimated below as 24 males (D in Table 15). In the CSDD, the use of principal offences leads to the concept of recidivism as 'the probability of reconviction following a criminal justice system intervention'. In the PYS data, separate court appearances at the same age cannot be identified, and recidivism is therefore calculated as 'the probability that an individual with n convictions will have at least one more'. The dual-*risk* recidivism model (Eq. (1)) was fitted to the data in Table 10; the parameter values are listed in Table 11; and the fitted curves and data are plotted in Figure 10. Again, the fit is very good for both the PYS cohorts, with well over 99 per cent of the variance accounted for.

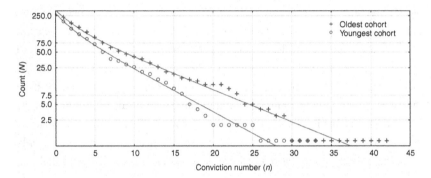

Figure 10 Count (*N*) of offenders with *n* or more convictions versus conviction number (*n*) in the PYS

Table 11 Parameter estimates for the dual-*risk* model

Data	Cohort prevalence	*A*	*a*	p_1	p_2	Variance explained
PYS youngest	39%	196	0.66	0.83	0.56	99.8%
PYS oldest	46%	235	0.60	0.87	0.62	99.8%
CSDD	43%	177	0.73	0.84	0.24	99.8%
OI 1953 cohort	37%	9,399	0.27	0.84	0.35	99.9%

Notes: A = number of first convictions, a = proportion of *high-risk* offenders, p_1 = *high-risk* probability of reconviction, and p_2 = *low-risk* probability of reconviction.

The parameter value differences between the two PYS cohorts are, to a certain extent, as expected, as longer observation periods would tend to reduce the

proportion of *high-risk* individuals[12] '*a*' whilst increasing the recidivism probabilities 'p_1' and 'p_2'. Counting all offences rather than principal offences (at each
court appearance) would also tend to increase the recidivism probability
estimates,[13] particularly for the *low-risk* category, when compared to the CSDD.
The estimates of the proportion *high-risk* '*a*' is similar between the PYS and CSDD
samples, perhaps reflecting the similar demographics in South London and inner-
city Pittsburgh. Demographic and period effects (see Fabio et al., 2006; MacLeod
et al., 2012, p. 45) also impact the cohort's prevalence of criminality. The estimates
of the probability of reconviction p_1, for the *high-risk* category, are remarkably
consistent across all cohorts (ranging 0.83–0.87). However, the estimates of the
probability of reconviction p_2 for the *low-risk* category are significantly higher for
the PYS cohorts than for the CSDD or OI cohorts, in part due to counting **all**
convictions in the PYS rather than just principal offences as in the CSDD and OI.

There are a number of deaths and emigrations recorded for the PYS cohort
members. From the youngest cohort, 17 died and 4 emigrated, and from the
oldest cohort, 26 died and 3 emigrated. Eight from the youngest and 10 from
the oldest cohort died or emigrated without being convicted, and although some
might have become late-onset offenders, they do not affect the *risk/rate* analysis
conducted here. Those with convictions, who died or emigrated, have only
a limited impact on the *risk* analysis but potentially do affect the *rate* analysis.

5.3 PYS *Rate* Analysis

Fitting the dual-rate survival model to the PYS data is less straightforward than
for the CSDD because the inter-conviction time can only be calculated as the
difference in age between successive convictions, which in the PYS data is
measured in whole years. Thus, two separate convictions at the same age would
result in zero inter-conviction time, and separate convictions just before and just
after a birthday would result in an inter-conviction time of one year. This coarse
measurement will result in errors in the individual inter-conviction times, but
because of the random nature of convictions relative to birthdays, these errors will
tend to cancel out when aggregated as survival time counts in a survival analysis.
If this were not the case, we might expect more erratic survival time curves than
those found (see later). Also, counting multiple offences at a single court appearance as separate convictions will inflate the zero inter-conviction time count.

Of the 21 males in the youngest cohort who died or emigrated, 13 were
convicted. As with the CSDD analysis, the probability of each of the 13

---

[12] Late-onset offenders are more likely to be *low-risk*.
[13] Without detailed information on multiple convictions at each court appearance in the PYS,
reconviction probabilities are not directly comparable with those in the CSDD.

individuals being convicted beyond their conviction-free time, if they had not died or emigrated, can be calculated from the *risk* and *rate* models. The sum of these probabilities provides an estimate of the potential number of false survivors, $F = 0.89$. Similarly, of 29 males in the oldest cohort who died or emigrated, 19 were convicted. The probabilities of each of the 19 individuals being convicted beyond their conviction-free periods were also calculated and summed to give an estimate of false survivors, $F = 1.38$.

Censorship is evident in the youngest cohort data, for survival times greater than twelve years. This has been modelled by modifying Eq. (2) to include the expected number of false survivors, F, and the censorship term 'D', which is the expected number of inter-conviction times greater than the maximum recorded in the follow-up period. Eq. (2) becomes:

$$S(t) = (S0 + D) * \left(b * e^{-\lambda_1 * t} + (1 - b) * e^{-\lambda_2 * t} \right) - D + F. \tag{7}$$

The estimated number of false survivors F was added explicitly prior to the estimation of the parameters b, λ_1, λ_2, and D.

In the analysis of the CSDD data, we have employed the concept of a conviction occasion, in which multiple offences at a single court appearance are counted as just one conviction. In the Pittsburgh data, we cannot isolate conviction occasions, and therefore, zero inter-conviction times could be the result of either multiple offences at one court appearance or separate offences at different court appearances at the same age. As a result, the reconviction probability estimates will be higher, and the mean inter-conviction time estimates will be shorter, in the PYS. In the PYS data, both conviction and reconviction counts will be affected. However, the numbers surviving to the next conviction beyond a birthday, by one, two, three, or more years, would not be affected, but the number at the start of the survival process would be. In the CSDD and OI analyses, S_0 was set explicitly to the total number of principal convictions recorded for the cohort. In the PYS, Eq. (7) has been fitted twice in both cohorts, first by setting S_0 to the total number of reconvictions and second by restricting the data to inter-conviction times greater than or equal to one year and including S_0 as a parameter in the fitting procedure. The results are shown in Table 12.

The restricted data estimates of S_0 suggest that for the oldest cohort, up to 339 of the 1,095 convictions could be multiple offences at a conviction occasion, but for the youngest cohort, few, if any, of the 707 convictions are multiples. For the youngest cohort, the rate parameters are unchanged by the 'restricted data' fit. However, for the oldest cohort the rate parameter values are reduced: for the *high-rate* category from 1.93 ± 0.08 down to 1.25 ± 0.14 convictions per year and for the *low-rate* category from 0.25 ± 0.01 down to 0.22 ± 0.01 convictions per year.

Table 12 Comparison of parameter estimates for the dual-*rate* survival model

	PYS youngest		PYS oldest		CSDD	OI (1953 cohort)
	Full data estimate	Restricted data estimate	Full data estimate	Restricted data estimate	estimate	estimate
S_0	*707*	708	*1,095*	756	826	*18,183*
b	0.66	0.66	0.73	0.66	0.62	0.56
λ_1	1.64	1.63	1.93	1.25	0.85	0.85
λ_2	0.27	0.27	0.25	0.22	0.16	0.21
D	2.35	2.36	0.04	1.69	–	–
F	*0.89*	*0.89*	*1.38*	*1.38*	2.99	–

Notes: b = the proportion of *high-rate* reconviction times, λ_1 = *high-rate* number of reconvictions per year, λ_2 = *low-rate* number of reconvictions per year, D = number of reconvictions expected beyond the observation period, and F = expected number of false survivors. The numbers in italics are set explicitly from the data. All other numbers are estimated by the fitting procedures.

Since the estimates in each pair are outside the confidence bounds of the other, these are statistically significant differences.

For the oldest PYS cohort, the restricted data fit not only reduces S_0, the total number of reconvictions, but also provides a better fit for survival times greater than twelve years. Figure 11 shows the data and the fitted curves; the dotted line is the restricted data fit to the oldest cohort data. The reduced proportion of *high-rate* (*b*) in the oldest cohort is consistent with the youngest cohort estimate and closer to that of the CSDD. The *high-rate* parameter λ_1 is reduced significantly, but this reflects the absence of very short inter-conviction times in the restricted data; λ_2 is less affected, with only a small reduction. The impact of the different parameter estimates was explored and is discussed later. Ultimately, it was decided that the full data estimates provided the best overall fit in the age–conviction analysis.

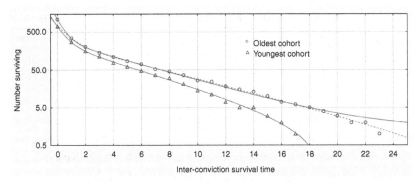

Figure 11 Number of inter-conviction times >*x* years for the PYS cohorts

Comparing the rate model parameter values across all cohorts, PYS, CSDD, and OI (Table 12), suggests quite remarkable consistency when considering the disparate nature of the samples (a sample from the whole population of England and Wales from the OI, an inner-city white working-class sample from South London from the CSDD, and an inner-city mixed-race working-class sample, with just over half being African American, from Pittsburgh in the PYS). The proportion of *high-rate* recidivists is slightly higher in the PYS than in the two UK samples. *High-rate* recidivists are convicted at around twice the rate in the PYS compared to the CSDD and OI samples, but the *low-rate* parameter, λ_2, is remarkably similar across all samples. It should be noted here that conviction rates are influenced by police/prosecution policy and practice as well as by offending frequency.

There is insufficient information available to resolve the issue of multiple offences at the same court appearance, and thus, the reconviction probability estimates, p_1 and p_2, for the PYS oldest cohort cannot be adjusted. Both the full data and restricted data estimates, for λ_1 and λ_2, were used in the allocation calculations to enable comparisons to be made in the age–conviction analysis. Applying the allocation procedures outlined in the appendix to MGF (2012, pp. 215–217), the number and proportion of offenders in each *risk/rate* category was calculated for all cohorts (see Table 13).

Table 13 Allocation of offenders to the *risk/rate* categories

	High-risk							
	PYS youngest		**PYS oldest**		**CSDD**		**OI**	
High-rate	96	49%	120	51%	81	46%	339	8%
Low-rate	33	17%	21	9%	48	27%	609	19%
	Low-risk							
	PYS youngest		**PYS oldest**		**CSDD**		**OI**	
Low-rate	67	34%	94	40%	48	27%	5558	73%
Cohort total	196	100%	235	100%	177	100%	6506	100%

The smaller proportion of *low-risk* offenders in the PYS youngest cohort is to be expected, as late-onset offenders are more likely to be *low-risk*. The proportion of *high-risk* offenders is reasonably consistent in the CSDD and PYS cohorts, but over twice that of the whole population sample from the OI, reflecting the higher criminality in inner-city samples. This also accounts for the much higher proportion of *low-risk* offenders in the OI sample.

5.4 PYS Age–Conviction Analysis

Table 14 lists the number of first and all convictions at each age for the PYS cohorts. It can be seen that the peak ages for first convictions were 13–16 and the peak ages for all convictions were 15–16, for both the youngest and oldest cohorts.

Using the rate parameter estimates listed in Table 12, the survival to first conviction model (Eq. (3)) was fitted to the data[14] for the PYS youngest and oldest cohorts. However, because of the shorter follow-up period for the PYS cohorts, the fitting procedure was modified to explicitly estimate the number of *low-rate* offenders who might be convicted for the first time beyond the data extent (D in Table 12), based on the search date of 2012. The survival curves for the youngest and oldest cohorts are plotted in Figure 12. The survival model

---

[14] First conviction data is unaffected by the multiple conviction issue.

Table 14 Count of first and all convictions at each age for the PYS cohorts

PYS youngest

Age	10	11	12	13	14	15	16	17	18	19	20
First conviction	3	5	15	26	27	18	25	6	18	9	6
All convictions	8	8	23	65	79	97	103	46	88	82	50

Age	21	22	23	24	25	26	27	28	29	30	31
First conviction	4	6	3	6	3	–	6	1	4	–	2
All convictions	44	47	28	26	26	13	20	11	31	6	2

PYS oldest

Age	10	11	12	13	14	15	16	17	18	19	20
First conviction	1	1	17	26	35	37	18	13	7	8	9
All convictions	11	15	65	152	198	184	168	99	79	72	61

Age	21	22	23	24	25	26	27	28	29	30	31
First conviction	5	2	3	2	1	1	2	–	–	2	1
All convictions	38	37	36	29	28	23	21	19	11	5	1

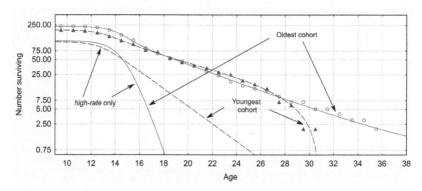

Figure 12 Survival to first conviction for PYS cohorts
Note: Logarithmic *y*-axis

parameter estimates are listed in Table 15. Again over 99 per cent of the variance in the survival data was accounted for in both PYS cohorts.

Table 15 Parameter estimates for survival to first conviction model (PYS)

	PYS youngest	PYS oldest	CSDD	OI
α	1.25	1.08	0.954	0.540
c	12.68	14.82	13.43	14.68
P_f	0.25	0.83	0.565	0.510
D	35	−0.5	−	−

Notes: α = slope of the rise in crime transition, c = midpoint age of the rise in crime transition, P_f = relative probability of a first conviction, and D = number of men who might be convicted for the first time beyond the data extent. Negative values of D suggest that all first convictions predicted by the model have occurred.

The estimates of the parameters c and P_f are different between the PYS cohorts, as is the estimate of D. The difference in the parameter estimates is clearly visible in the slope of the curves between ages 14 and 25 (see Figure 12). The shallower slopes of the youngest compared to the oldest cohort curves represent later ages of first conviction in the youngest cohort. The *high-rate* component of the model is plotted separately (curves in the lower left of the graph) and shows an even more marked difference in slope between the cohorts. The higher rate of first conviction may help explain the higher peak in first convictions and the lower levels of late onset found in the oldest PYS cohort.

The PYS rate and survival to first conviction model parameter estimates from Tables 11 and 15, and the category allocation proportions from Table 13 were substituted in Eq. (4) and summed over the *rate* categories to calculate the theoretical age at first conviction curves for the PYS cohorts. The curves and data are plotted in Figure 13(a) and 13(b). Using the 'full data' estimates to fit the theoretical model for age at first conviction provides a good fit to the data for both PYS cohorts, with virtually all data points lying within the $\pm 2\sigma$ bounds, the dotted lines on the graphs.[15]

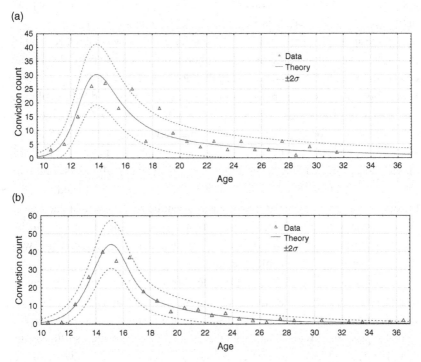

Figure 13 Age at first conviction for PYS cohorts: (a) youngest cohort and (b) oldest cohort

The two PYS cohorts are different from each other. The prevalence of convictions up to age 32 is significantly different, at the $p = 0.05$ level, between cohorts ($x^2 = 4.62$; 1 d_f; $p = 0.03$). For the youngest cohort 196 of 503 (39 per cent) were convicted, and for the oldest cohort, 231 of 506 (46 per cent) were convicted (OR = 1.32). In Figure 12, the differing slopes in the survival to first conviction curves, for *high-rate* category offenders, show that those in the oldest cohort tended to receive their first conviction earlier than those in the youngest cohort, prior to age 18 in the oldest and age 26 in the youngest. Parameter D, the expected number of late-onset offenders, is also very different. For the oldest cohort, $D = -0.5 \pm 1.75$, close to zero, which

---

[15] The $\pm 2\sigma$ confidence interval assumes a Poisson distribution about the modelled value.

implies that all potential offenders have been convicted by age 38. However, for the youngest cohort $D = 24 \pm 8$, which suggests that there are between 16 and 32 potential late-onset offenders who might be convicted beyond age 32. If the estimates of the Ds are correct, then the prevalence of conviction, in the long term, might be similar in both cohorts. The number of reconvictions is over 25 per cent higher in the oldest cohort, even allowing for censorship at different ages (32 and 38 for the youngest and oldest cohorts, respectively), and the peak in the age–conviction curve is 30 per cent higher in the oldest cohort.

Demographics can explain some of the differences between the UK and US samples but not between the two PYS cohorts. It is of course possible that the cohorts are simply different, but given that both are from the same neighbour-hoods and same schools, explanations for these differences need to be explored. The initial screening was conducted between ages 5 and 9 (mean age = 7, $\pm 2 * \sigma = \pm 1.1$) for the youngest cohort and between ages 11 and 15 (mean age = 13, $2 * \sigma = 1.6$) for the oldest cohort. The samples are biased in favour of those who are most likely to become *high-risk* category offenders, one half selected as potentially *high-risk* and one half randomly selected. In addition, for the oldest cohort, the screening took place when the males could already have been criminally active. Therefore, we would expect cohort criminality to be high and late-onset offenders to be under-represented if the initial screening was effective, particularly in the oldest cohort.

A change in prosecution policy for under 18s at about the time the youngest cohort reached the age of criminal responsibility might help explain the differ-ences. Police and prosecutors have discretion as to which offences, if any, are formally proceeded with. Warnings or cautions may be deemed sufficient for first offences, and less serious offences may not be proceeded with where more serious offences have been committed. The parameter P_f represents the prob-ability of formal proceedings, given no previous serious criminal involvement. For the oldest cohort, $P_f = 0.83$, but for the youngest cohort, P_f is less than half that at 0.34. One possible explanation for this change is a relaxation in the policy governing the decision to charge first offenders, resulting in a delay in first convictions. This is clearly seen in Figure 12, particularly for the *high-rate* category offenders, where the theoretical curves show no first convictions beyond age 18 for the oldest cohort, compared with age 22 for the youngest cohort. Could early convictions account for the difference in the estimated numbers of late-onset offenders? Early first convictions would lead to early reconvictions, albeit with the same inter-conviction time distributions, an earlier peak in the age–conviction curve for all convictions and earlier termination, but probably with the same career duration. This latter conjecture relies on the proposition that it is the formal intervention of the criminal justice system that encourages the decision to desist from crime.

Substituting the parameter values for p_1, p_2, λ_1, λ_2, and the *risk/rate* proportions, from Tables 11–13, in Eqs. (5) and (6), and summing over the *risk/rate* categories for the youngest and oldest PYS cohorts generate the theoretical age–conviction profiles plotted in Figure 14 with ±2σ bounds. In these graphs, the data are plotted as stacked histograms, with 'in-age' reconvictions (reconviction time = 0) on top of 'other' convictions (convictions with reconviction time > 0) in the middle and 'first' convictions on the bottom. Identifying these different types of convictions highlights the extent to which multiple offences, on a single conviction occasion, might have affected the data.

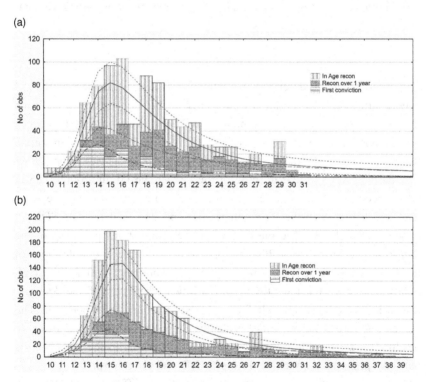

Figure 14 Age–conviction curves for PYS cohorts: (a) youngest and (b) oldest

In both the youngest and oldest cohorts, around 25 per cent of data points lie outside the theoretical confidence interval, mostly above the +2σ curve. This was not the case with first convictions, where all except two data points from the youngest cohort were contained within these limits, and none of the data points in the oldest cohort lay outside the respective ±2σ confidence intervals. The lower two dotted line curves in Figure 14(a) and 14(b) are the theoretical age at 'first' and 'first' plus 'reconviction time ≥1' convictions, and both curves follow the data quite closely. First convictions and consecutive convictions at different ages (i.e. with reconviction time, as measured in the PYS, ≥1) must necessarily be separate conviction occasions.

The disjunction between the theoretical model and the data clearly arises from reconvictions. The number of 'in-age' reconvictions is much greater than expected from the theory and again suggests multiple offences on a single court appearance rather than separate offences on different court appearances. The observed numbers of in-age reconvictions, most notably in the oldest cohort for age groups 13 to 17, suggests a policy of maximising charges. In addition, the parameter P_f is close to 1, indicating that most offending is treated formally rather than using warnings or cautions, as in the UK samples.

5.5 Conclusions

The *risk/rate* model, described in Section 2 and developed for the OI 1953 cohort, fitted the PYS criminal career data for both cohorts very well: the number of males with *n* or more convictions, time intervals between convictions, the age–crime curve, and the age at first conviction curve. Remarkably, the risks of recidivism of the *high-risk* categories of both PYS cohorts were very similar to those of the CSDD and OI, at around 0.85 in all four cohorts. However, the risks of recidivism of the *low-risk* categories were much higher in the PYS cohorts (around 0.6) than in the CSDD/OI cohorts (around 0.3). The rates of offending (convictions per year) of the *high-rate* categories in the PYS cohorts were both around double those of the OI and CSDD cohorts: 1.64 for the PYS youngest, 1.93 for the PYS oldest, and 0.85 for the OI/CSDD. However, the rates of the *low-rate* categories were similar in all four cohorts, at around 0.25 per year. The higher PYS risks and rates are probably caused by counting all offences resulting in a conviction at the same court appearance in the PYS cohorts but only principal convictions in the CSDD and OI cohorts.

The present section also sheds more light on the differences in offending between the PYS cohorts. It was previously noted that the oldest cohort included a higher proportion of offenders (Fabio et al., 2006), but the present analyses provide additional insights into the precise nature of these cohort differences. Next, Section 6 investigates the extent to which the PYS offenders in different *risk/rate* categories could be predicted by childhood and early teenage risk factors.

6 Childhood Prediction of *Risk/Rate* Categories in the PYS

The models developed from the MacLeod et al. theory (Eqs. (1) and (2)) were successfully applied to the reconviction data from the youngest and oldest cohorts of the PYS in Section 5. Again, with allowances made for differences between the cohorts in demographics and data collection, the PYS model parameters were found to be quite consistent with those of the UK cohorts. The PYS also collected extensive personal information on the cohort members at annual intervals.

6.1 Allocating Cases to *Risk/Rate* Categories

Following the procedures outlined in Section 4 convicted cohort members were allocated to retrospectively defined *risk/rate* categories (HH, HL, and LL) and the NC category. Because inter-conviction times are measured as integer years, inter-conviction times are calculated as age differences between the first and last convictions divided by conviction count minus 1. The uncertainty between multiple convictions at a single court appearance and separate convictions at the same age means that the risk cut points were not as clearly defined as in the CSDD data. The cut points chosen were those which resulted in *risk* allocations closest to the theoretical estimates.

For the youngest cohort, individuals with one conviction and, for the oldest cohort, those with one or two convictions, were designated as *low risk*, resulting in 55 and 85 cases, respectively. The rate cut points were chosen as those which resulted in rate allocations closest to the theoretical estimates. It was also assumed that all offenders designated as *low-risk* were also *low-rate*. Those designated as *high-rate* had average inter-conviction time greater than zero and less than 2.59 years for the oldest cohort and average inter-conviction times greater than zero and less than 2.20 years for the youngest cohort. The resulting retrospective *risk/rate* allocations are given in Table 16. Again, there is some misallocation compared with the MacLeod et al. theoretical predictions, made worse by the data problems described previously. In particular, the *LL* category is underestimated, while the *HL* category is overestimated in the youngest cohort; *HH* and *LL* are underestimated; and *HL* is overestimated in the oldest cohort.

Table 16 Comparison of theoretical *risk/rate* category allocations with retrospective allocations for the PYS data

risk/rate category	Theoretical *HH*	Data HH	Theoretical *HL*	Data HL	Theoretical *LL*	Data LL
Youngest cohort	96	97	33	44	67	55
Oldest cohort	120	110	39	49	93	85

6.2 PYS Risk Factors

In selecting risk factors from the PYS, the aim was to select 25 important risk factors that were as comparable as possible to those measured in the CSDD. This was not so difficult because, in many ways, the particular risk factors that were initially measured in the PYS were inspired by results previously obtained in the CSDD, since David Farrington – the director of the CSDD – was co-principal investigator of the PYS from its inception in 1986–1987. As in the CSDD, the PYS risk factors were dichotomized (where possible) into the 'worst' quarter versus the remainder when they were not naturally dichotomous (e.g. a broken family).

Farrington and Loeber (1999) carried out a systematic comparison of CSDD and PYS risk factors for delinquency and found many similarities. Among the most important risk factors in both studies were hyperactivity, low school achievement, poor parental supervision, an antisocial parent, a young mother, large family size, low family income, and a broken family. Where there were differences, they were explainable. For example, physical punishment was a much stronger predictor in the CSDD, probably because it included a cold, rejecting attitude. It is possible that physical punishment in the PYS was sometimes given in the context of a loving relationship. Low socio-economic status (SES) was a much stronger predictor in the PYS, possibly because it included parental education as well as employment but also because there were well-paid manual jobs (e.g. printers and dockers) in London in the 1960s that were not available in Pittsburgh in the 1980s. More recently, Zych et al. (2021) reported that, over twenty explanatory risk factors, PYS effect sizes (based on the logarithm of the odds ratios) correlated 0.58 with CSDD effect sizes.

The twenty-five PYS risk factors studied in this section were drawn from those included in the third PYS book by Loeber and Farrington (2011); for more information about them, see also the first and second PYS books (Loeber et al., 1998, 2008). They were measured in the first two waves of the PYS (the screening wave and the first follow-up wave) when the youngest cohort were mostly aged 7–8 and the oldest cohort were mostly aged 13–14. Table 2.3 of the 2011 book lists fifty-three risk factors (excluding measures of offending). All risk factors with more than 10 per cent missing cases in either cohort (e.g. father's behaviour problems, bad neighbourhood according to census data) were excluded, and then the most important and most comparable twenty-five PYS risk factors were chosen. They are as follows:

Parental: Most risk factors were based on the mother's report. Police contacts of relatives referred to any relative (parents, aunts and uncles, or siblings) who had contact with the police because of their criminal behaviour. A young mother identified mothers who were teenagers at the time of their first birth. Parent substance use identified a parent who had sought help for alcohol or drug problems. Parent stress reflected parents who were having difficulties in dealing with life's problems.

Family: Physical punishment was based on information from the mother and the boy about whether the mother slapped, spanked, or hit the boy if he did something wrong. Poor parental supervision was based on the same sources and reflected whether the parent knew what the boy was doing when he was outside the home. A bad relationship with the parent was based on the same sources. A broken family was derived from the mother's report and identified families with at least one missing biological parent.

Socio-economic: A small house was based on the mother's report, and it referred to homes with less than six rooms (including kitchens and bathrooms). The family on welfare was also based on the mother's report, as was an unemployed mother, which referred to being unemployed for at least a quarter of the time in the previous six months. Large family size was based on the boy's report of the number of children living in the home, and boys living with three or more other children were considered to be in a large family. Low SES was based on a combination of the education and employment of the parents, according to the mother's report. A bad neighbourhood was based on the mother's report of problems in the neighbourhood, such as vandalism, racial conflict, and disrespect for authority.

Attainment: Low attainment was measured by the California Achievement Test and by mother–teacher ratings on the CBCL and the Teacher Report Form. Whether the boy was old for the grade (because he had to repeat a grade) was based on the mother's report.

Personality: Callous-unemotional personality was based on the Teacher Report Form, reflecting factors such as teasing a lot and an explosive or unpredictable personality. Hyperactivity-impulsivity-attention (HIA) problems were based on mother–teacher ratings on the CBCL and the Teacher Report Form, of the boy's impulsiveness, difficulty in concentrating, and so on. Depressed mood was based on the boy's report on the Recent Mood and Feelings Questionnaire, of feeling unhappy, unloved, and so on. Lack of guilt was based on mother–teacher ratings, while bad friends were based on mother and boy information about the boy having friends who were a bad influence on him.

Behaviour: Disruptive behaviour disorder was derived from the Diagnostic Interview Schedule for Children (DISC-P), completed by the mother, and referred to the boy meeting the Diagnostic and Statistical Manual of Mental Disorders, Third Edition (DSM-IIIR) criteria for attention-deficit hyperactivity disorder, conduct disorder, or oppositional defiant disorder. The boy's cruelty to people was rated by the mother and teacher on the CBCL and the Teacher Report Form. Whether the boy had been suspended from school was based on information from the mother and the boy.

6.3 Risk Factors Predicting *Risk/Rate* Categories in the PYS Youngest Cohort

For the youngest cohort, Table 17 shows the risk factor predictions of each *risk/rate* category (HH, HL, or LL); the category allocations are all compared with those who were not convicted. The first column shows the risk factors, followed by three sets of three columns showing the proportions allocated with risk factor = yes (% R), with risk factor = no (% NR) and the odds ratios with statistical significance indicated by significant $**p < 0.05$ and near-significant $*p < 0.1$, for each of the allocated categories.

The strongest predictors of HH males were: broken family (OR = 4.62), parent substance use (OR = 3.89), callous-unemotional (OR = 3.59), family on welfare (OR = 3.52), cruel to people (OR = 3.44), suspended from school (OR = 3.22), young mother (OR = 2.80), low SES (OR = 2.51), large family size (OR = 2.45), police contact of relatives (OR = 2.31), bad neighbourhood (OR = 2.17), low attainment according to parent and teacher (OR = 2.07), old for grade (OR = 2.01), low CAT (OR = 1.98), parental stress (OR = 1.96), lack of guilt (OR = 1.92), HIA (OR = 1.88), and unemployed mother (OR = 1.86).

The strongest predictors of HL males were: callous-unemotional (OR = 4.49), cruel to people (OR = 4.15), depressed mood (OR = 3.90), low attainment according to parent and teacher (OR = 3.77), family on welfare (OR = 3.66), HIA (OR = 3.2), lack of guilt (OR = 3.06), suspended from school (OR =2.88), bad neighbourhood (OR = 2.83), low CAT (OR = 2.70), physical punishment (OR = 2.60), low SES (OR = 2.49), young mother (OR = 2.37), disruptive behaviour (OR = 2.27), broken family (OR = 2.23), poor supervision (OR = 2.20), large family size (OR = 2.16), unemployed mother (OR = 2.08), bad relationship with parent (OR = 2.07), and parent substance use (OR = 2.02).

There were the same numbers (twenty) of significant predictors of HL males and HH males, while there were thirteen significant predictors of LL males. The strongest predictors of LL males were: HIA (OR = 3.09), a bad relationship with parent (OR = 3.07), a young mother (OR = 2.63), low SES (OR = 2.58), large family size (OR = 2.46), low attainment according to parent and teacher (OR = 2.37), low attainment on the CAT (OR = 2.06), callous-unemotional

Table 17 PYS youngest cohort risk factors predicting *risk/rate* categories

	HH			HL			LL		
	% R	% NR	OR	% R	% NR	OR	% R	% NR	OR
Parental									
Police contact of relatives	33.1	17.7	2.31**	16.8	11.2	1.61	16.1	15.1	1.08
Parent substance use	42.3	15.8	3.89***	20.0	11.0	2.02**	18.8	13.7	1.47
Young mother	39.7	19.1	2.80**	22.6	11.0	2.37***	26.8	12.2	2.63**
Parent stress	33.0	20.1	1.96**	16.5	12.0	1.44	21.1	13.3	1.74*
Family									
Physical punishment	25.0	23.2	1.10	23.8	10.7	2.60**	21.3	14.0	1.66
Poor supervision	24.7	23.2	1.09	21.2	10.9	2.20**	23.0	12.9	2.01**
Bad relationship with parent	32.6	21.0	1.81**	20.5	11.1	2.07***	28.4	11.4	3.07***
Broken family	32.6	9.5	4.62**	16.8	8.3	2.23**	18.9	10.6	1.96**
Socio-economic									
Small house	31.1	20.9	1.71**	17.0	12.0	1.50	18.9	14.0	1.43
Family on welfare	35.8	13.6	3.52***	21.8	7.1	3.66**	20.1	11.4	1.96**
Unemployed mother	32.6	20.7	1.86***	20.5	11.0	2.08**	22.5	13.0	1.94***
Large family size	38.2	20.1	2.45**	21.7	11.3	2.16***	26.6	12.8	2.46**
Low SES	37.4	19.2	2.51**	22.5	10.4	2.49**	26.2	12.1	2.58**
Bad neighbourhood	35.1	19.9	2.17**	23.8	9.9	2.83**	22.8	13.1	1.95**
Attainment									

Table 17 (cont.)

	HH			HL			LL		
	% R	% NR	OR	% R	% NR	OR	% R	% NR	OR
Low CAT	35.2	21.6	1.98**	24.6	10.8	2.70**	24.6	13.7	2.06**
Low attainment (PT)	34.9	20.6	2.07**	27.3	9.1	3.77**	25.3	12.5	2.37**
Old for grade	35.8	21.8	2.01**	8.1	13.6	0.56	17.1	15.0	1.17
Personality									
Callous–unemotional	45.7	19.0	3.59**	30.2	8.8	4.49**	22.8	12.8	2.02*
HIA	34.5	21.9	1.88***	28.0	10.6	3.29**	30.8	12.6	3.09**
Depressed mood	28.4	22.3	1.38	27.5	8.9	3.90**	20.5	13.9	1.60
Lack of guilt	33.8	21.0	1.92**	25.4	10.0	3.06**	22.1	13.7	1.78*
Bad friends	26.8	22.2	1.28	17.2	11.5	1.60	18.0	14.2	1.33
Behaviour									
Disruptive behaviour	30.1	21.8	1.54	21.6	10.8	2.27**	21.6	13.6	1.75*
Cruel to people	43.5	18.3	3.44**	29.4	9.1	4.15***	21.3	14.0	1.67
Suspended from school	42.9	18.9	3.22**	25.4	10.6	2.88***	18.5	14.7	1.32

Notes: OR = odds ratio, R = risk, NR = non-risk, PT = parent–teacher rating, and CAT = California Achievement Test.

personality (OR = 2.02), and poor supervision (OR = 2.01). The family on welfare, a young mother, low SES, a bad neighbourhood, large family size, and a bad relationship with the parent were predictors of all *risk/rate* categories. Physical punishment was a predictor only of HL males.

6.4 Logistic Regression Analyses (PYS Youngest Cohort)

Following the procedures described in Section 4 for the CSDD cohort, to investigate which risk factors predicted the *risk/rate* categories of offenders independently of other risk factors, logistic regression analyses were carried out. It is important to investigate independent predictors because, of course, some of the risk factors are related to other risk factors (especially to those in the same category). For example, a callous-unemotional personality was significantly related to lack of guilt (OR = 6.9) and hyperactivity (OR = 3.6), and the family on welfare was related to an unemployed mother (OR = 4.6), low SES (OR = 3.5), and a bad neighbourhood (OR = 3.8).

Because of our interest in identifying explanatory risk factors, the behavioural risk factors (disruptive behaviour disorder, cruel to people, and suspended from school) were excluded from these analyses. It seems likely that these risk factors are measuring the same underlying construct as offending (e.g. a criminal or antisocial personality); therefore, the fact that they predict offending probably does not reflect any kind of causal effect on offending but merely the persistence of this underlying construct.

First, we entered all the significant predictors in a forward stepwise logistic regression to see which ones came out as significant (or near-significant) independent predictors. After this first analysis, we continued entering significant (and near-significant) predictors from each regression in further regressions until the final model was clear.

Table 18 shows the results of the logistic regression analyses. The strongest independent predictors of the HH category were a callous-unemotional personality, parent stress, police contact of relatives, a bad neighbourhood, large family size, a young mother, low SES, and an unemployed mother. These eight predictors were drawn from four different risk factor groups: parental, family, personality, and socio-economic.

The strongest predictors of the HL group were a callous-unemotional personality, a depressed mood, the family on welfare, a bad relationship with the parent, large family size, and a young mother. These predictors were drawn from four risk factor groups: personality, socio-economic, family, and parental. Three of these

Table 18 Results of logistic regression analyses (PYS youngest cohort)

	LRCS	*P*	POR	*P*
High-risk/high-rate (*N* = 329)				
Callous-unemotional	21.99	0.0001	4.85	0.0001
Parent stress	14.78	0.0001	2.79	0.0007
Police contact of relatives	11.76	0.0003	2.97	0.0002
Bad neighbourhood	10.29	0.0007	2.22	0.008
Large family size	7.21	0.004	2.50	0.005
Young mother	8.62	0.002	2.53	0.006
Low SES	3.55	0.030	1.73	0.047
Unemployed mother	2.48	0.058	1.71	0.056
High-risk/low-rate (*N* = 298)				
Callous-unemotional	20.50	0.0001	4.09	0.0002
Depressed mood	11.43	0.0004	3.22	0.001
Family on welfare	8.47	0.002	2.29	0.023
Bad relationship with parent	3.74	0.027	2.46	0.015
Large family size	3.67	0.028	2.66	0.018
Young mother	2.12	0.073	1.98	0.069
Low-risk/low-rate (*N* = 340)				
Bad relationship with parent	12.86	0.0002	2.96	0.001
Large family size	7.91	0.002	3.03	0.002
Young mother	8.68	0.002	3.02	0.002
HIA	6.86	0.004	2.82	0.005
Unemployed mother	2.60	0.054	1.79	0.051

Notes: LRCS = likelihood ratio chi-squared improvement, POR = partial odds ratio, and *p* values one-tailed

six predictors (large family size, a callous-unemotional personality, and a young mother) were among the strongest predictors of the HH category.

The strongest predictors of the LL category were a bad relationship with the parent, large family size, a young mother, HIA, and an unemployed mother. Three of these (large family size, young mother, and unemployed mother) were among the best independent predictors of the HH category. Again, these predictors were drawn from only the parental, family, socio-economic, and personality risk factor groups. Attainment factors were not important predictors of any of these three *risk/rate* categories.

6.5 Prospective Identification of *Risk/Rate* Categories in the PYS Youngest Cohort

By coding the risk factors 1 = risk and 0 = non-risk, scores were created for each male in the youngest cohort by summing over the significant risk factors listed in Table 18. A score was created for each of the *risk/rate* categories (HH, HL, and LL). The scores were used in an ROC analysis comparing each category with the NC males. The resulting plots of true positive rate versus false positive rate are shown in Figure 15.

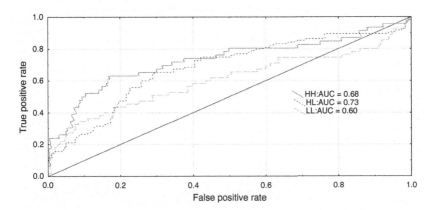

Figure 15 ROC curves for HH versus NC, HL versus NC, and LL versus NC, PYS youngest cohort

The AUC provides a measure of the probability that two individuals, chosen at random, would be ranked correctly by the score for the respective *risk/rate* category. The AUCs were 0.68, 0.73, and 0.60 for the HH, HL, and LL categories, respectively. This is a similar result to that obtained with the CSDD cohort, with the same caveat regarding the retrospective identification of categories and the selective comparisons.

Valid category factor scores were calculated for 409 HH, 424 HL, and 470 LL of the 503 youngest cohort members. Figure 16 shows the probability of category membership versus each of the category factor scores. For all of the category factor scores, the higher the score, the more likely it is that the outcome would be allocation to one of the *risk/rate* categories.

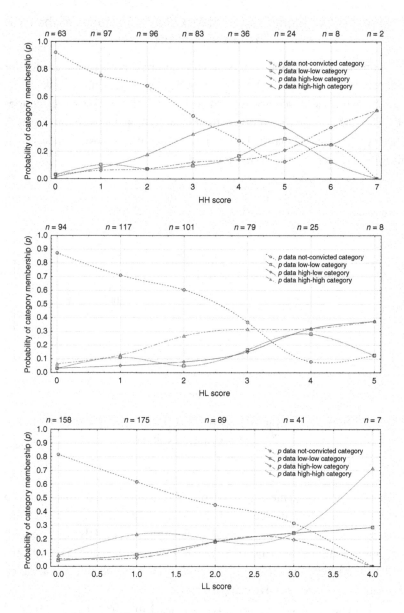

Figure 16 Probability of retrospective-category allocation for each category factor score, PYS youngest cohort

6.6 Risk Factors Predicting *Risk/Rate* Categories in the PYS Oldest Cohort

Table 19 shows the risk factor predictions of each *risk/rate* category (HH, HL, or LL); the category allocations are all compared with NC. The first column shows

Table 19 Risk factors predicting *risk/rate* categories in the PYS oldest cohort

	HH			HL			LL		
	% R	% NR	OR	% R	% NR	OR	% R	% NR	OR
Parental									
Police contact of relatives	32.1	26.5	1.31	16.0	9.6	1.81	26.4	21.5	1.32
Parent substance use	33.3	22.2	1.75**	15.4	10.1	1.61	22.4	24.4	0.89
Young mother	48.2	22.2	3.27***	18.5	10.5	1.95*	33.3	22.5	1.73*
Parent stress	41.3	23.6	2.28***	16.4	11.0	1.59	29.9	21.9	1.52
Family									
Physical punishment	37.5	26.5	1.67*	16.7	11.4	1.55	30.8	22.4	1.54
Poor supervision	44.0	22.9	2.65***	12.5	12.6	1.00	29.1	22.0	1.45
Bad relationship with parent	43.3	24.1	2.41**	20.3	10.5	2.17**	31.1	21.9	1.61*
Broken family	36.1	12.1	4.11**	15.3	7.6	2.18**	25.1	22.1	1.18
Socio-economic									
Small house	41.3	24.5	2.17**	17.0	11.4	1.59	34.3	21.6	1.90**
Family on welfare	47.3	17.8	4.14***	20.0	9.6	2.36**	35.2	17.1	2.64**
Unemployed mother	40.2	25.7	1.95**	21.0	10.2	2.33**	34.7	21.3	1.96**
Large family size	35.5	26.5	1.53*	16.7	11.3	1.56	25.0	23.6	1.08
Low SES	41.5	24.3	2.21**	22.5	9.3	2.84**	32.1	21.5	1.72*

Table 19 (cont.)

	HH			HL			LL		
	% R	% NR	OR	% R	% NR	OR	% R	% NR	OR
Bad neighbourhood	42.2	24.1	2.30**	16.1	11.1	1.55	33.3	21.4	1.84**
Attainment									
Low CAT	41.0	20.3	2.73**	20.3	8.0	2.94**	28.9	20.6	1.57
Low attainment (PT)	46.8	22.9	2.96**	25.4	9.0	3.43**	24.2	23.7	1.03
Old for grade	42.6	21.1	2.77**	18.8	9.8	2.13**	31.0	20.5	1.74**
Personality									
Callous-unemotional	45.9	21.6	3.08**	20.7	7.6	3.18**	29.2	23.0	1.38
HIA	50.7	24.1	3.24**	25.0	10.5	2.85**	31.3	22.7	1.55
Depressed mood	33.7	27.1	1.37	10.9	13.0	0.83	28.8	22.4	1.40
Lack of guilt	54.8	20.4	4.75**	27.6	8.5	4.12**	31.1	22.5	1.56
Bad friends	46.2	23.2	2.84**	16.9	11.6	1.56	39.5	19.3	2.74**
Behaviour									
Disruptive behaviour	47.3	22.5	3.09**	21.0	9.8	2.43**	31.9	21.7	1.69*
Cruel to people	57.5	20.3	5.29**	28.8	9.3	3.97**	33.9	21.9	1.83*
Suspended from school	41.9	7.9	8.36**	18.4	4.8	4.48**	31.1	14.7	2.61**

Notes: OR = odds ratio, R = risk, NR = non-risk, PT = parent–teacher rating, and CAT = California Achievement Test the risk factors, followed by three sets of three columns showing the proportion allocated with risk factor = yes (% R), with risk factor = no (% NR) and the odds ratios, with statistical significance indicated by significant ** = $p < 0.05$ and near-significant * = $p < 0.1$, for each of the allocated categories.

The strongest of the twenty-one significant predictors of HH males were suspended from school (OR = 8.36), cruel to people (OR = 5.29), lack of guilt (OR = 4.75), the family on welfare (OR = 4.14), a broken family (OR = 4.11), a young mother (OR = 3.27), HIA (OR = 3.24), disruptive behaviour (OR = 3.09), a callous-unemotional personality (OR = 3.08), low attainment according to parent and teacher (OR = 2.96), bad friends (OR = 2.84), old for grade (OR = 2.77), low attainment on the CAT (OR = 2.73), poor supervision (OR = 2.65), a bad relationship with parents (OR = 2.41), a bad neighbourhood (OR = 2.30), parental stress (OR = 2.28), low SES (OR = 2.21), and a small house (OR = 2.17).

The strongest predictors of HL males were suspended from school (OR = 4.48), lack of guilt (OR = 4.12), cruel to people (OR = 3.97), low attainment according to parent and teacher (OR = 3.43), a callous-unemotional personality (OR = 3.18), low attainment on the CAT (OR = 2.94), HIA (OR = 2.85), low SES (OR = 2.84), disruptive behaviour (OR = 2.43), the family on welfare (OR = 2.36), an unemployed mother (OR = 2.33), a broken family (OR = 2.18), a bad relationship with parents (OR = 2.17), and old for grade (OR = 2.13).

The strongest predictors of LL males were bad friends (OR = 2.74), the family on welfare (OR = 2.64), and suspended from school (OR = 2.61). Family on welfare, suspended from school, and an unemployed mother were significant predictors of all *risk/rate* categories. All fourteen significant predictors of HL males were among the twenty-one significant predictors of HH males.

6.7 Logistic Regression Analyses (PYS Oldest Cohort)

Following the same procedures applied to the CSDD cohort and the PYS youngest cohort, to investigate which risk factors predicted the *risk/rate* categories of offenders independently of other risk factors, logistic regression analyses were carried out. As before, the behavioural risk factors (disruptive behaviour disorder, cruel to people, and suspended from school) were excluded from these analyses.

First, we entered all the significant predictors in a forward stepwise logistic regression to see which ones came out as significant (or near-significant) independent predictors. After this first analysis, we continued entering significant (and near-significant) predictors from each regression in further regressions until the final model was clear.

Table 20 shows the results of the logistic regression analyses. The strongest independent predictors of the HH category were: a lack of guilt, a young mother,

Table 20 Results of logistic regression analyses (PYS oldest cohort)

	LRCS	*P*	POR	*P*
***High-risk/high-rate** (N = 342)*				
Lack of guilt	39.94	0.0001	3.88	0.0001
Young mother	17.03	0.0001	3.32	0.0001
Bad friends	9.34	0.001	2.29	0.004
Unemployed mother	7.17	0.004	1.84	0.031
Low SES	5.00	0.013	1.73	0.038
Small house	3.61	0.029	1.89	0.031
Bad relationship with parent	2.41	0.060	1.73	0.047
Bad neighbourhood	1.72	0.095	1.53	0.093
***High-risk/low-rate** (N = 277)*				
Lack of guilt	14.39	0.0001	4.43	0.0001
Young mother	3.06	0.040	2.06	0.048
Family on welfare	2.22	0.068	1.81	0.066
***Low-risk/low-rate** (N = 332)*				
Family on welfare	12.67	0.0002	2.32	0.001
Bad friends	9.18	0.001	2.30	0.003
Small house	2.8	0.047	1.75	0.043
Bad relationship with parent	1.77	0.092	1.53	0.089

Notes: LRCS = likelihood ratio chi-squared improvement, POR = partial odds ratio, and *p* values one-tailed.

bad friends, an unemployed mother, low SES, a small house, a bad relationship with the parent, and a bad neighbourhood. These predictors were drawn from five different risk factor groups: parental, family, socio-economic, peer, and personality (all except attainment).

The strongest predictors of the *HL* category were similar. Lack of guilt and a young mother were again the strongest predictors, followed by the family on welfare. These predictors were drawn from only three risk factor groups: family, socio-economic, and personality.

The strongest predictors of the *LL* category were: the family on welfare, bad friends, a small house, and a bad relationship with the parent. Three of these (all except the family on welfare) were among the best independent predictors of the HH category. Again, these predictors were drawn from only the family, socio-economic, peer, and personality risk factor groups. Attainment and parental risk factors were not important predictors of the LL category, or of the HH category.

6.8 Prospective Identification of *Risk/Rate* Categories in the PYS Oldest Cohort

As previously mentioned, the risk factors were coded 1 = risk and 0 = non-risk, and scores were created for each male in the oldest cohort by summing over the significant risk factors listed in Table 20. For example, an individual who showed a lack of guilt in a family on welfare would have an HL score of 2. For each individual valid scores were created for each of the *risk/rate* categories (HH, HL, and LL). Valid scores require all contributing significant factors to be valid. Of the 506 oldest cohort members, 465 had a valid HH score, 448 had a valid HL score and 469 had a valid LL score. The scores were used in an ROC analysis comparing each category with the NC males.

The resulting plots of true positive rate versus false positive rate are shown in Figure 17, The AUCs are a little higher for the HH and LL categories (0.70 and 0.64) than obtained in the youngest cohort (0.68 and 0.60) but lower for the HL category (0.65 for the oldest cohort compared with 0.70 for the youngest). However, the HH, HL, and LL categories are nevertheless correctly identified with probabilities between 0.65 and 0.70. This is again a similar result to that obtained with the CSDD cohort but with the same caveat regarding the retrospective identification of categories and the selective comparisons.

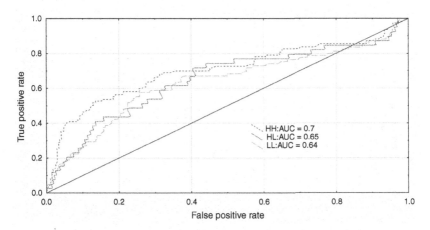

Figure 17 ROC curves for HH versus NC, HL versus NC, and LL versus NC, PYS oldest cohort

Figure 18 shows the probability of allocated *risk/rate* category membership versus each of the category factor scores. For all of the category factor scores, the higher the score, the more likely it was that the outcome would be allocation to one of the *risk/rate* categories.

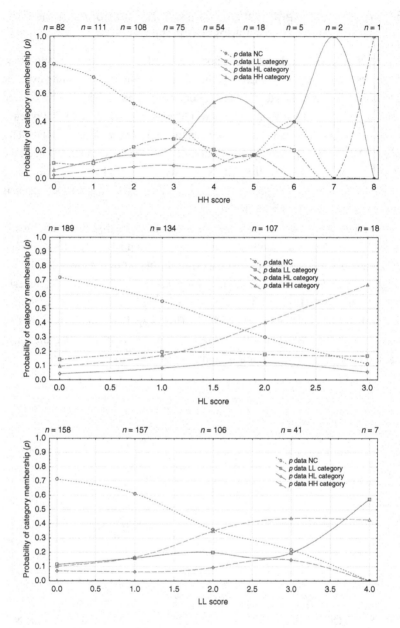

Figure 18 Probability of retrospective-category allocation for each category factor score, PYS oldest cohort

6.9 Conclusions

These analyses show the extent to which HH, HL, and LL males could be predicted in the two PYS cohorts from early risk factors. Once again, this is a step towards expanding our simple theory (which predicts criminal career features) into a more complex theory that specifies the influence of risk factors. The results are consistent with the CSDD, in that the prediction scores all show an increasing probability of membership of one of the *risk/rate* categories with increasing scores. Of the variables that were found to be significant predictors of the risk/rate categories, only large family size has directly equivalent measures in both the CSDD and the PYS data sets. For the PYS, police contact of relatives, a broken home, and a small house are similar constructs to a convicted father, a disrupted family, and poor housing, respectively, in the CSDD. Attainment, intelligence, and poor supervision were important predictors in the CSDD but did not feature in the PYS, despite having direct equivalents in both data sets. Similarities and differences between the predictors of HH, HL, and LL males in all cohorts are discussed in Section 7.

7 Final Conclusions

The main aim of our Element, as stated in Section 1, is to make progress towards scientific criminological theories that make quantitative predictions about criminal career features such as the prevalence and frequency of offending at different ages. As mentioned, most criminological theories only aim to explain the prevalence of offending and do not make or test quantitative predictions. The starting point for our theory and analyses is the simple mathematical model developed by Barnett et al. (1987). This focussed on only two variables – the frequency of offending and the probability of reoffending – but it could quantitatively predict some key criminal career features. Barnett et al. (1987) identified two categories of offenders: frequents (with a high frequency of offending and a high probability of reoffending) and occasionals (with a lower frequency of offending and a lower probability of reoffending). They could not fit the data by assuming that all offenders had the same frequency of offending and the same probability of reoffending.

7.1 Testing the Theory

In Section 2, we described key features of the theory and research of MacLeod et al. (2012). This theory also focussed on the key parameters (which are meaningful) of the frequency (*rate*) of offending and the probability (*risk*) of reoffending. Both parameters were assumed to be constant over time. However, MacLeod et al. (2012) proposed three categories of offenders: those with a *high risk* and a *high rate* (*HH*), those with a *high risk* and a *low rate* (*HL*), and those with a *low risk* and a *low rate* (*LL*). There was no evidence of the possible fourth category (*low risk and high rate*) in the large national (English) data sets that they analysed. In the section, we also showed how the MacLeod et al. (2012) theory could fit the observed age–crime curve for both first and all convictions. It is important to note that each of the propositions of the theory relates directly to the parameters of the model, and all of the parameters are potentially measurable in the real world.

In Section 3, this theory was applied to the CSDD data. There were more *HH* males (46% vs 19%) and *HL* males (27% vs 8%) in the CSDD than in the national data, no doubt because the CSDD was based in an inner-city working-class area. However, the *high-risk* probability of reoffending (0.84) was the same in the CSDD and national data, while the low-risk probabilities were not very different (0.24 in the CSDD and 0.35 in the national data). Also, the *high-rate* frequency of offending was similar in the CSDD and national data (0.87 vs 0.85 offences per year), as was the *low-rate* frequency of offending (0.17 vs 0.21 offences per year). This simple theory closely fitted the CSDD criminal career data: the number of males with n or more convictions, time intervals between convictions, the age–crime curve, and the age at first conviction curve.

The same theory was then applied (in Section 5) to the youngest and oldest cohorts of the PYS. The *risk/rate* model fitted the PYS criminal career data for both cohorts very well: the number of males with n or more convictions, time intervals between convictions, the age–crime curve, and the age at first conviction curve. The proportion of *HH* males in the youngest (49%) and oldest (51%) PYS cohorts was similar to the proportion (46%) in the CSDD. However, there were fewer *HL* males in the youngest (17%) and oldest (9%) PYS cohorts than in the CSDD (27%). Conversely, there were slightly more *LL* males in the youngest (34%) and oldest (40%) PYS cohorts than in the CSDD (27%).

Remarkably, the high-risk probabilities of reoffending in the youngest (0.83) and oldest (0.87) PYS cohorts were very similar to the CSDD figure (0.84). However, the low-risk probabilities of reoffending were higher in the youngest (0.56) and oldest (0.62) PYS cohorts than in the CSDD (0.24). The *high-rate* frequencies of offending were much higher in the youngest (1.64 per year) and oldest (1.93 per year) PYS cohorts than in the CSDD (0.85 per year). However, the *low-rate* frequencies of offending were not much higher in the youngest (0.27 per year) and oldest (0.25 per year) PYS cohorts than in the CSDD (0.16 per year). These differences were explained by the fact that all offences leading to convictions were counted in the PYS, while only the most serious offence on each conviction occasion was counted in the CSDD.

The accuracy of prediction of criminal career features in several data sets provides considerable support for the propositions of the simple theory. The fact that the probability of reconviction is constant over time might imply that a conviction is an important factor in the offender's decision to desist from crime. If this is correct, then improving clearance rates, by catching and convicting offenders more quickly, should reduce overall crime rates.

7.2 Risk Factors for HH, HL, and LL Males

Section 4 aimed to extend the theory by investigating childhood (age 8–10) risk factors in the CSDD that predicted the HH, HL, and LL males (compared with NC males). The strongest independent predictors of HH males were drawn from five different risk factor categories: parental (a convicted father), family (a disrupted family), socio-economic (poor housing), attainment (low attainment and low non-verbal IQ), and personality (high daring). These variables were often among the strongest predictors of offending in previous CSDD analyses.

In contrast, the strongest predictors of HL males were drawn from only three categories: family (poor parental supervision, a disrupted family), socio-economic (poor housing and large family size), and attainment (low attainment). While parental (a convicted father) and personality (high daring) factors were the strongest independent predictors of HH males, they were not among the strongest independent predictors of HL males. There were only three significant independent predictors of LL males, drawn from three categories: parental (a convicted father), family (a disrupted family), and socio-economic (poor housing). Attainment and personality factors were not important predictors of LL males.

Risk scores were then calculated, based on the significant independent predictors. For the prediction of HH, HL, and LL males, the AUCs were 0.72, 0.64, and 0.64, respectively. These AUC values indicate moderate to good predictability. As explained in the Element, perfect prediction would not be expected because the theory would specify that a certain fraction of true *HH* males would be falsely identified as HL or LL males (and a corresponding statement would apply to the true *HL* and *LL* males).

There were some similarities and some differences between the predictors of HH, HL, and LL males. In particular, a disrupted family and poor housing were independent predictors of all three categories, whereas a convicted father predicted only the HH and LL categories. However, low non-verbal IQ and high daring were unique predictors of the HH category, while large families and poor supervision were unique predictors of the HL category. These results suggest how the basic theory might be extended to propose particular risk factors that influence the development of particular categories of offenders.

Section 6 aimed to extend the theory by investigating childhood and adolescent risk factors in the PYS youngest and oldest cohorts that predicted HH, HL, and LL males (compared with NC males). We made big efforts to choose PYS risk factors that were comparable to the CSDD risk factors but there were inevitably some differences: for example, there was no exactly comparable measure in the PYS to a convicted father in the CSDD, and there was no comparable measure in the CSDD to bad friends in the PYS. Table 21 shows the strongest predictors in the PYS, compared with the CSDD. It can be seen that large family size and a young mother predicted all three categories in the youngest cohort, whereas no single variable predicted all three categories in the oldest cohort (although a young mother predicted HH and HL males). A young mother seemed to be more important in the PYS than in the CSDD. Attainment, intelligence, and poor supervision were important predictors in the CSDD but did not feature in the PYS, despite having direct equivalents in both data sets.

In the youngest cohort, a callous-unemotional personality predicted the HH and HL males, but this variable was not an independent predictor in the oldest cohort. In the youngest cohort, a bad relationship with the parent predicted HL and LL males, and this variable also predicted HH and LL males in the oldest cohort. In the oldest cohort, lack of guilt predicted HH and HL males, but this variable was not an independent predictor in the youngest cohort. Similarly, bad friends and a small house predicted HH and LL males in the oldest cohort, but these variables were not independent predictors in the youngest cohort. A bad neighbourhood and low SES predicted HH males in both cohorts but neither of the other two categories.

As for the CSDD, risk scores were calculated in all cases for the PYS, and AUC values were in the range of 0.60–0.70, indicating moderate to good predictability.

Based on the current state of knowledge, it is difficult for us to explain all the results shown in Table 21. The variables are all important and well-known risk factors for later offending. More research would be needed to establish the extent to which the predictors of HH, HL, and LL males were similar or different. In general, there were more independent predictors of HH males than of HL or LL males. The main predictors of HL and LL males in both cohorts were family and socio-economic factors, while the main predictors of HH males in both cohorts were parental, personality, family, and socio-economic factors.

Our analyses, however, do suggest ways in which criminological theories might be extended to include risk factors in exact quantitative predictions of criminal career features. The first step would probably be to study one summary variable from each of the risk factor categories and test postulates about how these risk factors are quantitatively related to categories of offenders. The main problem is that the number of parameters of the theory could increase quickly, suggesting that a cautious stepwise approach would be advisable, always

Table 21 Independent predictors of HH, HL, and LL males

CSDD	PYS youngest	PYS oldest
HH	**HH**	**HH**
Convicted father	Callous-unemotional	Lack of guilt
High daring	Parent stress	Young mother
Low attainment	Police contact of relatives	Bad friends
Disrupted family	Bad neighbourhood	Unemployed mother
Poor housing	Large family size	Low SES
Low non-verbal IQ	Young mother	Small house
	Low SES	Bad relationship with parent
	Unemployed mother	Bad neighbourhood
HL	**HL**	**HL**
Poor supervision	Callous-unemotional	Lack of guilt
Large family size	Depressed mood	Young mother
Disrupted family	Family on welfare	Family on welfare
Low attainment	Bad relationship with parent	
Poor housing	Large family size	
	Young mother	
LL	**LL**	**LL**
Convicted father	Bad relationship with parent	Family on welfare
Poor housing	Large family size	Bad friends
Disrupted family	Young mother	Small house
	HIA	Bad relationship with parent
	Unemployed mother	

Note: HIA = hyperactivity-impulsivity-attention deficit

assessing whether the increase in predictive power outweighs the increased complexity of the theory.

7.3 The Next Generation of Criminal Career Theories

In our opinion, the ideal theory is a simple theory that explains (and quantitatively fits) a wide range of criminal career findings. We believe that our criminal career theory is this type of theory. We first propose two major and meaningful parameters – the probability of recidivism after an offence (*risk*) and the frequency of offending by offenders (*rate*) – and assume that they are constant and invariant with age. Then we assume that there are two categories of offenders with different risks and two categories with different rates. These assumptions generate a theory with six parameters: *high risk* probability, *low risk* probability, prevalence of *high risk* (vs *low risk*), *high rate* (convictions per year), *low rate*, and prevalence of *high rate* (vs *low rate*). With this simple theory, we have shown that we can accurately and quantitatively fit a wide range of criminal career data, including the crucial feature of the age–crime curve (the number of offenders and offences at each age), inter-conviction intervals, and the probability of recidivism after each offence.

This theory generates four possible categories of offenders: *high-risk/high-rate, high-risk/low-rate, low-risk/high-rate*, and *low-risk/low-rate*. As we have not found any evidence of the *low-risk/high-rate* category, our theory only includes the other three categories of offenders. We have also tried to investigate which risk factors influence which categories of offenders. We hope that we have made some progress towards the next generation of criminal career theories, which should accurately and quantitatively predict not only crucial criminal career features but also the strength of relationships between risk factors and types of offenders. In turn, this knowledge should lead to more effective prevention methods that target key risk factors.

For example, consider the very influential theory of Moffitt (1993), described in Section 1. She focussed primarily on two types of offenders: LCP and AL, allegedly influenced by different risk factors. Most of the well-known classic risk factors were assumed to influence the LCP offenders. Later, Moffitt added the categories of low-level chronics and abstainers (non-offenders). We think that it would be desirable for Moffitt to try to measure the rate of offending and the risk of reoffending in her criminal career data from New Zealand. Ideally, she should estimate the six parameters specified above (separately for males and females). We believe that this could enable her to exactly predict the prevalence and frequency of offending by her male and female cohorts at different ages, based on different types of offenders.

It is possible that her LCP offenders would turn out to be HH or HL offenders, while her low-level chronics might turn out to be HL or LL offenders. We are not sure whether her AL offenders might be a mixture of all types of offenders, but it would be interesting to study this. Alternatively, Moffitt could propose a more complex theory, where the AL offenders have a high probability of recidivism up to a certain age (e.g. 20 or 25) and then a lower probability of recidivism afterwards. The key empirical question would be whether any benefits from increased predictive accuracy outweighed the costs of the increased complexity of the theory. This kind of cost-benefit decision could be made for all theories. It would also be interesting for Moffitt to study the relationships between early risk factors and types of offenders, once again to develop quantitative predictions of key criminal career features.

We suggest that other major theories in developmental and life-course criminology (see e.g. Farrington, 2005) could be similarly developed to yield exact quantitative predictions of key criminal career features. For example, the ICAP theory (Farrington, 2020a), like many other theories, does not propose that there are types of offenders. Instead, it suggests that all offenders vary on the continuous underlying dimension of antisocial potential, which is influenced by specified individual, family, and socio-economic risk factors. It would be possible to compare the predictive accuracy of a theory assuming a continuous underlying rate of offending with our theory that proposes only two rate categories (*H* and *L*). Again, the key empirical question would be whether any benefits from increased predictive accuracy outweighed the costs of the increased complexity of the theory.

Most criminal career research, as in this Element, is based on official records. The challenge for criminologists is to develop and test theories that also explain and predict self-reported offending at different ages.

7.4 Implications for Theory and Policy

When more adequate scientific criminological theories have been developed and tested, they should provide useful information about how to invest resources in crime prevention most efficiently. For example, it would be most beneficial to prevent the development of HH offenders. High daring in the CSDD and a callous-unemotional personality and lack of guilt in the PYS were important predictors of these, and these personality problems might be efficiently prevented using cognitive-behavioural skills training programmes (Zara, 2019). Similarly, low attainment was an important predictor of HH males in the CSDD, and this could be targeted in preschool intellectual enrichment programmes (Zych & Farrington, 2019). Another important predictor was socio-economic deprivation: poor housing in the CSDD and a bad neighbourhood, unemployed mother, and low SES in the PYS. This could perhaps be targeted by vocational training or a programme such as 'Moving to Opportunity' (Ludwig et al., 2013).

In conclusion, we have shown how simple theories can accurately predict and explain important criminal career features, and we have also shown how these simple theories could be extended by studying how early risk factors influence types of offenders. Quantitative theories and models are important in criminology as they permit better forecasting and planning in the criminal justice system and indicate which policy interventions might be most cost-effective.

We encourage criminologists to build on our research and develop and test more scientific and quantitative theories of criminal careers. We hope that our simple theory will inspire a new generation of theories that make and test quantitative predictions about key criminal career features and that specify quantitative relationships between risk factors and types of offenders.

References

Ahonen, L., Farrington, D. P., Pardini, D. A. & Stouthamer-Loeber, M. (2021). Cohort profile: The Pittsburgh Youth Study (PYS). *Journal of Developmental and Life-Course Criminology*, 7, 481–523.

Ahonen, L., FitzGerald, D., Klingensmith, K. & Farrington, D. P. (2020). Criminal career duration: Predictability from self-reports and official records. *Criminal Behaviour and Mental Health*, 30, 172–182.

Barnett, A., Blumstein, A. & Farrington, D. P. (1987). Probabilistic models of youthful criminal careers. *Criminology*, 25, 83–107.

Barnett, A., Blumstein, A. & Farrington, D. P. (1989). A prospective test of a criminal career model. *Criminology*, 27, 373–388.

Barnett, A. & Lofaso, A. J. (1985). Selective incapacitation and the Philadelphia cohort data. *Journal of Quantitative Criminology*, 1, 3–36.

Blumstein, A., Cohen, J. & Farrington, D. P. (1988a). Criminal career research: Its value for criminology. *Criminology*, 26, 135.

Blumstein, A., Cohen, J. & Farrington, D. P. (1988b). Longitudinal and criminal career research: Further clarifications. *Criminology*, 26, 57–74.

Blumstein, A., Cohen, J., Roth, J. A. & Visher, C. A. (Eds.) (1986). *Criminal careers and 'career criminals'*, 2 Vols. Washington, DC: National Academy Press.

Blumstein, A., Farrington, D. P. & Moitra, S. (1985). Delinquency careers: Innocents, desisters, and persisters. In M. Tonry & N. Morris (Eds.), *Crime and justice*, Vol. 6 (pp. 187–222). Chicago: University of Chicago Press.

Fabio, A., Loeber, R., Balasubramani, G. K. et al. (2006). Why some generations are more violent than others: Assessment of age, period and cohort effects. *American Journal of Epidemiology*, 164, 151–160.

Farrington, D. P. (1986). Age and crime. In M. Tonry & N. Morris (Eds.), *Crime and justice*, Vol. 7 (pp. 189–250). Chicago: University of Chicago Press.

Farrington, D. P. (1992). Criminal career research in the United Kingdom. *British Journal of Criminology*, 32, 521–536.

Farrington, D. P. (1995). The development of offending and antisocial behaviour from childhood: Key findings from the Cambridge Study in Delinquent Development. *Journal of Child Psychology and Psychiatry*, 36, 929–964.

Farrington, D. P. (2003). Key results from the first 40 years of the Cambridge Study in Delinquent Development. In T. P. Thornberry & M. D. Krohn (Eds.),

Taking stock of delinquency: An overview of findings from contemporary longitudinal studies (pp. 137–183). New York: Kluwer/Plenum.

Farrington, D. P. (Ed.) (2005). *Integrated developmental and life-course theories of offending (Advances in Criminological Theory*, Vol. 14). New Brunswick: Transaction.

Farrington, D. P. (2019). The Cambridge Study in Delinquent Development. In D. Eaves, C. D. Webster, Q. Haque & J. Eaves-Thalken (Eds.), *Risk rules: A practical guide to structured professional judgment and violence prevention* (pp. 225–233). Hove: Pavilion.

Farrington, D. P. (2020a). The Integrated Cognitive Antisocial Potential (ICAP) theory: Past, present, and future. *Journal of Developmental and Life-Course Criminology*, 6, 172–187.

Farrington, D. P. (2020b). Childhood risk factors for criminal career duration: Comparisons with prevalence, onset, frequency, and recidivism. *Criminal Behaviour and Mental Health*, 30, 159–171.

Farrington, D.P. (2021). New findings in the Cambridge Study in Delinquent Development. In J.C. Barnes & D.R. Forde (Eds.) *The encyclopedia of research methods in criminology and criminal justice* (vol. 1, pp. 96–103). Hoboken: Wiley.

Farrington, D. P., Coid, J. W. & West, D. J. (2009). The development of offending from age 8 to age 50: Recent results from the Cambridge Study in Delinquent Development. *Monatsschrift fur Kriminologie und Strafrechtsreform (Journal of Criminology and Penal Reform)*, 92, 160–173.

Farrington, D. P. & Hawkins, J. D. (1991). Predicting participation, early onset, and later persistence in officially recorded offending. *Criminal Behaviour and Mental Health*, 1, 133.

Farrington, D. P., Jolliffe, D. & Coid, J. W. (2021). Cohort profile: The Cambridge Study in Delinquent Development (CSDD). *Journal of Developmental and Life-Course Criminology*, 7, 278–291.

Farrington, D. P., Langan, P. A. & Tonry, M. (Eds.) (2004). *Cross-national studies in crime and justice*. Washington, DC: U.S. Bureau of Justice Statistics (NCJ 200988).

Farrington, D. P. & Loeber, R. (1999). Transatlantic replicability of risk factors in the development of delinquency. In P. Cohen, C. Slomkowski & L. N. Robins (Eds.), *Historical and geographical influences on psychopathology* (pp. 299–329). Mahwah: Lawrence Erlbaum.

Farrington, D. P. & Loeber, R. (2000). Some benefits of dichotomization in psychiatric and criminological research. *Criminal Behaviour and Mental Health*, 10, 100–122.

Farrington, D. P., MacLeod, J. F. & Piquero, A. R. (2016). Mathematical models of criminal careers: Deriving and testing quantitative predictions. *Journal of Research in Crime and Delinquency, 53,* 336–355.

Farrington, D. P., Piquero, A. R. & Jennings, W. G. (2013). *Offending from childhood to late middle age: Recent results from the Cambridge Study in Delinquent Development.* New York: Springer.

Farrington, D. P. & West, D. J. (1981). The Cambridge Study in Delinquent Development (United Kingdom). In S. A. Mednick & A. E. Baert (Eds.), *Prospective longitudinal research* (pp. 137–145). Oxford: Oxford University Press.

Farrington, D. P. & West, D. J. (1990). The Cambridge Study in Delinquent Development: A long-term follow-up of 411 London males. In H.-J. Kerner & G. Kaiser (Eds.), *Kriminalitat: Personlichkeit, lebensgeschichte und verhalten (Criminality: Personality, behavior and life history)* (pp. 115–138). Berlin: Springer-Verlag.

Gibson, H. B. (1967). Teachers' ratings of schoolboys' behaviour related to patterns of scores on the New Junior Maudsley Inventory. *British Journal of Educational Psychology, 37,* 347–355.

Gottfredson, M. R. & Hirschi, T. (1986). The true value of lambda would appear to be zero: An essay on career criminals, criminal careers, selective incapacitation, cohort studies, and related topics. *Criminology, 24,* 213–234.

Hirschi, T. & Gottfredson, M. R. (1983). Age and the explanation of crime. *American Journal of Sociology, 89,* 552–584.

Jennings, W. G., Loeber, R., Pardini, D., Piquero, A., & Farrington, D. P. (2016). *Offending from childhood to young adulthood: Recent results from the Pittsburgh Youth Study.* New York: Springer.

Loeber, R., Ahonen, L., Stallings, R. & Farrington, D. P. (2017). Violence de-mystified: Findings on violence by young males in the Pittsburgh Youth Study. *Canadian Psychology, 58,* 305–315.

Loeber, R. & Farrington, D. P. (2011). *Young homicide offenders and victims: Risk factors, prediction, and prevention from childhood.* New York: Springer.

Loeber, R., Farrington, D. P., Stouthamer-Loeber, M. & Van Kammen, W. B. (1998). *Antisocial behavior and mental health problems: Explanatory factors in childhood and adolescence.* Mahwah: Lawrence Erlbaum.

Loeber, R., Farrington, D. P., Stouthamer-Loeber, M. & White, H. R. (2008). *Violence and serious theft: Development and prediction from childhood to adulthood.* New York: Routledge.

Loeber, R., Stouthamer-Loeber, M., Van Kammen, W. B. & Farrington, D. P. (1989). Development of a new measure of self-reported antisocial behavior for young children: Prevalence and reliability. In M. W. Klein (Ed.), *Cross-*

national research in self-reported crime and delinquency (pp. 203–225). Dordrecht: Kluwer.

Loeber, R., Stouthamer-Loeber, M. S., Van Kammen, W. & Farrington, D. P. (1991). Initiation, escalation, and desistance in juvenile offending and their correlates. *Journal of Criminal Law and Criminology*, 82, 36–82.

Ludwig, J., Duncan, G. J., Gennetian, L. A. et al. (2013). Long-term neighborhood effects on low-income families: Evidence from Moving To Opportunity. *American Economic Review*, 103, 226–231.

MacLeod, J. F., Grove, P. G. & Farrington, D. P. (2012). *Explaining criminal careers: Implications for justice policy*. Oxford: Oxford University Press.

McGee, T. R. & Moffitt, T. E. (2019). The developmental taxonomy. In D. P. Farrington, L. Kazemian & A. R. Piquero (Eds.), *The Oxford handbook of developmental and life-course criminology* (pp. 149–158). New York: Oxford University Press.

Ministry of Justice (2010). *Conviction histories of offenders between the ages of 10 and 52*. London: Ministry of Justice (Statistics Bulletin).

Moffitt, T. E. (1993). Adolescence-limited and life-course persistent antisocial behavior: A developmental taxonomy. *Psychological Review*, 100, 674–701.

Moffitt, T. E. (2006). Life-course persistent versus adolescence-limited antisocial behavior. In D. Cicchetti & D. J. Cohen (Eds.), *Developmental psychopathology*, Vol. 3 (pp. 570–598). New York: Wiley.

Moffitt, T. E. (2018). Male antisocial behaviour in adolescence and beyond. *Nature Human Behaviour*, 2, 177–186.

Nagin, D. S. (2005). *Group-based modeling of development*. Cambridge, MA: Harvard University Press.

Nagin, D. S. & Farrington, D. P. (1992). The stability of criminal potential from childhood to adulthood. *Criminology*, 30, 235–260.

Nagin, D. S., Farrington, D. P. & Moffitt, T. E. (1995). Life-course trajectories of different types of offenders. *Criminology*, 33, 111–139.

Nagin, D. S. & Land, K. C. (1993). Age, criminal careers, and population heterogeneity: Specification and estimation of a nonparametric, mixed Poisson model. *Criminology*, 31, 327–336.

Nagin, D. S. & Tremblay, R. E. (1999). Trajectories of boys' physical aggression, opposition, and hyperactivity on the path to physically violent and nonviolent juvenile delinquency. *Child Development*, 70, 1181–1196.

Nagin, D. S. & Tremblay, R. E. (2005). Developmental trajectory groups: Fact or a useful statistical fiction? *Criminology*, 43, 873–904.

Piquero, A. R., Farrington, D. P. & Blumstein, A. (2007). *Key issues in criminal career research: New analyses of the Cambridge Study in Delinquent Development*. Cambridge: Cambridge University Press.

Rocque, M., Posick, C. & Hoyle, J. (2016). Age and crime. In W. G. Jennings (Ed.), *The encyclopedia of crime and punishment* (pp. 1–4). New York: Wiley.

Skardhamar, T. (2010). Distinguishing facts and artifacts in group-based modeling. *Criminology*, 48, 295–320.

Theobald, D., Farrington, D. P., Loeber, R., Pardini, D. A. & Piquero, A. R. (2014). Scaling up from convictions to self-reported offending. *Criminal Behaviour and Mental Health*, 24, 265–276.

Weisburd, D., Braga, A. A., Groff, E. R. & Wooditch, A. (2017). Can hot spots policing reduce crime in urban areas? An agent-based simulation. *Criminology*, 55, 137–173.

West, D. J. (1969). *Present conduct and future delinquency*. London: Heinemann.

West, D. J. (1982). *Delinquency: Its roots, careers, and prospects*. London: Heinemann.

West, D. J. & Farrington, D. P. (1973). *Who becomes delinquent?* London: Heinemann.

West, D. J. & Farrington, D. P. (1977). *The delinquent way of life*. London: Heinemann.

Wikstrom, P.-O. H. & Treiber, K. (2019). The dynamics of change: Criminogenic interactions and life-course patterns in crime. In D. P. Farrington, L. Kazemian & A. R. Piquero (Eds.), *The Oxford handbook of developmental and life-course criminology* (pp. 272–294). New York: Oxford University Press.

Wolfgang, M. E., Figlio, R. M. & Sellin, T. (1972). *Delinquency in a birth cohort*. Chicago: University of Chicago Press.

Zara, G. (2019). Cognitive-behavioral treatment to prevent offending and to rehabilitate offenders. In D. P. Farrington, L. Kazemian & A. R. Piquero (Eds.), *The Oxford handbook of developmental and life-course criminology* (pp. 694–725). New York: Oxford University Press.

Zych, I. & Farrington, D. P. (2019). Developmental preschool and school programs against violence and offending. In D. P. Farrington, L. Kazemian & A. R. Piquero (Eds.), *The Oxford handbook of developmental and life-course criminology* (pp. 673–693). New York: Oxford University Press.

Zych, I., Farrington, D. P., Ribeaud, D. & Eisner, M. P. (2021). Childhood explanatory factors for adolescent offending: A cross-national comparison based on official records in London, Pittsburgh and Zurich. *Journal of Developmental and Life-Course Criminology*, 7, 308–330.

Acknowledgements

The CSDD was mainly funded by the Home Office and the Department of Health, with other funding from the Department of Education, the Rayne Foundation, the Barrow Cadbury Trust, and the Smith-Richardson Foundation. For carrying out CSDD criminal record searches, we are very grateful to Gwen Gundry in the 1960s and 1970s, Lynda Morley in the 1980s, Sandra Lambert in the 1990s, Debbie Wilson in the 2000s, Owen Thomas in 2011–2012, and Lisa Robinson in 2017. The PYS was mainly funded by the Office of Juvenile Justice and Delinquency Prevention, the National Institute of Mental Health, and the National Institute of Drug Abuse, with other funding from the Pew Charitable Trusts and the Pennsylvania Department of Health. We are very grateful to Rebecca Stallings for assembling the 2012 PYS convictions data set.

Cambridge Elements ≡

Criminology

David Weisburd
George Mason University, Virginia
Hebrew University of Jerusalem

Advisory Board

About the Series

Elements in Criminology seek to identify key contributions in theory and empirical research that help to identify, enable, and stake out advances in contemporary criminology. The series will focus on radical new ways of understanding and framing criminology, whether of place, communities, persons, or situations. The relevance of criminology for preventing and controlling crime will also be a key focus of this series.

Cambridge Elements $^{\equiv}$

Criminology

Elements in the Series

Developmental Criminology and the Crime Decline
Jason L. Payne, Alexis R. Piquero

A Framework for Addressing Violence and Serious Crime
Anthony A. Braga, David M. Kennedy

Whose 'Eyes on the Street' Control Crime? Expanding Place Management into Neighborhoods
Shannon J. Linning, John E. Eck

Confronting School Violence: A Synthesis of Six Decades of Research
Jillian J. Turanovic, Travis C. Pratt, Teresa C. Kulig, Francis T. Cullen

Testing Criminal Career Theories in British and American Longitudinal Studies
John F. MacLeod, David P. Farrington

A full series listing is available at: www.cambridge.org/ECRM

Printed in the United States
by Baker & Taylor Publisher Services